Rob Fijlstra and Harry Wullings are partners in the firm Fijlstra • Wullings in Amstelveen, The Netherlands. They are professionals with a mission. In their work they are concerned about what individuals and organizations can do to make better use of their potential and find a way to a more productive, pleasurable and creative future.

Working in the practical world of organizational development and training, they have developed into leading and authoritative consultants, trainers, speakers and authors, concentrating on leadership, inter-personal competencies, emotional intelligence, organizational development, and cultural and mind-change.

Rob Fijlstra is the writer in the duo. He delivers virtually one hundred percent of the *perspiration* that such an exercise demands, both mentally and physically. *Honesty: The Best Policy* has partly arisen thanks to the *inspiration* of his partner Harry Wullings. Much of the content has been gleaned from the experience and developments they have both experienced in their work over the years. This is good enough reason to put both their names on the cover of this book.

www.fijlstrawullings.nl
fw@fijlstrawullings.nl

HONESTY: THE BEST POLICY

A REMEDY AGAINST ALIENATION, CYNICISM AND POWERLESSNESS

ROB FIJLSTRA
HARRY WULLINGS

CYAN | SCRIPTUM

Translation: Jonathan Ellis & Amie de Jeu-Horwin

First published in the United Kingdom by
Cyan | Scriptum
A member imprint of Cyan Communications
Registered office: 61 Cooper Close
London SE1 7QU, United Kingdom
www.cyanbooks.com

ISBN 1-904879-14-4

Printed and bound in Belgium

CONTENTS

FOREWORD

"Simplicity is inexhaustible." – Krishnamurti

IN THIS BOOK we continue our search for authenticity and credibility in the behavior of individuals and organizations. We are constantly learning more about ourselves and our work. There is every reason to continue that search. Because who would dare claim perfection for themselves or for the organization for which they work? Reality shows that, while the outside world looks on in amazement, most organizations are managed with mediocrity and indifference. Which is why most people go onto automatic pilot the moment they enter the company compound.

We are searching for a new type of awareness. We have, it seems, the wind against us: on the seas of management fashion, it is the hierarchical world of thought, with its delusions of grandeur that is the constant winner on the organizational tides of evolution. It will hardly raise an eyebrow that so many embrace this way of thinking and hardly believe there is any alternative to it. And so the culture within most organizations is still firmly patriarchal and polarized.

And yet there is a growing awareness that the current problems cannot be solved at the same level of thinking that has created them (freely adapted from Einstein). There is the on-going danger of the emergence of a culture of greedy bartering and restitution, in which there is little room for real relationships and the underlying qualities of heart and mind. People lower their moral thresholds and concentrate on maximizing their own comfort and short-term profits. If that doesn't make enough money, then they start tampering with the figures and, in no time, immense conflicts arise and gross alienation. Until the ship flounders.

Anything that collapses makes the news. So it is not such a bad thing that organizations are brought down by their own paradoxes and dilemmas. For people, this development can cause considerable discomfort. Their job and their "belief in the company" are up for grabs. They feel as if they have been sold out and abandoned. This can lead to sadness and estrangement making it not easy to get your mind back on track.

Yet every painful experience can contribute to personal development or even accelerate that development. It only demands the courage to look the situation in the eye and take responsibility for your own part in the problem. When suddenly you are no longer the victim of external circumstances, the proper perspective frequently reveals itself.

It is all about trust in yourself; embracing, trusting, and valuing what is already there rather than searching for something new. Sometimes you have to distance yourself from something that doesn't work rather than taking refuge in self-deception and self-treason. We all need to do some self-reflection to learn to trust ourselves and be honest. Honesty with ourselves and others is the first step.

ACKNOWLEDGMENTS

It is encouraging to be surrounding by inspirational colleagues both at home and abroad who are part of the same wave of consciousness in thinking and acting. Companions and like thinkers, with the same ideals, the same dedication and the same question marks, desires, and hopes. And in this process, we share the same mission to shift boundaries wherever necessary. In this way, we each help the other to move another step forward.

The following people have most recently and identifiably helped us with our process of developing our awareness; this book is the result of this.

Aalt Aalten, who shows with his aikido approach how more can be achieved with less energy and that you do not need to damage somebody to remain on your own feet.

Ken Blanchard, always a source of inspiration thanks to his constant passion to create human organizations.

Geoffrey Bellman, who with his books and his consultancy work shows in a truly honest manner that inner civilization, consistent performance, and simplicity are the true strengths of a professional.

Peter Block, perhaps one of the most authentic thinkers of this time and a constant source of inspiration for thinking about individual and organizational development.

Arnold Cornelis, who unfortunately died much too young. With his books he enormously stimulated thinking about the "logic of emotional development."

Wessel Ganzevoort for his friendship and his inspiring and revealing contribution to the development of organizations and the people who work in them.

Joop Swieringa and Jacqueline Jansen, for their practical and theoretical contributions about the learning person and their sometimes deaf and dumb organizations.

André Wierdsma for his rich contribution to the profession and to finding the right words (co-creation).

Robert Quinn for his wonderful books *Deep Change* and *Change the World*.

Cees Zwart, who has given an enormous impulse to our thinking about course-searching leadership and humane organizations.

And of course the people at home are a constant source of new insights and jumps in awareness. In this important aspect of our lives, the term "love" finds its most tangible form and it highlights when we are being less than truthful. And it shows that terms such as love, faith and commitment know no nuances. In real life, there is no such thing as "a little bit in love." For love is nothing less than complete attention and care for the sometimes hidden possibilities within yourself and your partner. We hope our struggle for increased awareness will contribute to a decreasing gap between desire and reality in our closest relationships. In any case, Amke, Joke, and José are our constant support in this process. Amke, in particular, has, thanks to her loving tolerance of the consequences of writing this book, contributed to its completion.

This book is intended to provide a positive impulse to the reader's development process. The title *Honesty: The Best Policy* suggests a high and perhaps unattainable level of ambition. We are not perfect nor do we expect the reader to become so. Despite our intentions, we may find that this new way of thinking has occasionally not fully penetrated our behavior, or we simply do not have the courage to live with the consequences of our insights. Hopefully you will forgive us this, or at least tolerate it. After all, life is always "under construction," and for on-going development it is better to have something to wish for. We wish the reader much inspiration and pleasure.

Rob Fijlstra *&* Harry Wullings

THE URGENCY

"A Zen pupil was so zealously searching for enlightenment that he would sit and pray throughout the morning, afternoon, and evening. He hardly ever stopped to eat or sleep. His master saw him becoming weaker as each day passed and asked: 'Why do you neither eat nor take the rest that your body and soul deserve?' 'Because I want to become enlightened and I do not have a moment to waste.' The master answered: 'Why do you desire enlightenment so much? Maybe you may stray from what you seek because of this haste. Perhaps enlightenment lies behind you, and all you need to do is stand still so that this force can overtake you.'" – Source unknown

THE SPEED OF CHANGE is increasing and the technological possibilities are exploding. We have to do so much more in an ever-shorter time that we, to some extent, lose touch with the daily fundamentals of existence. But change is very much like the weather. Complaining doesn't help, so you might as well get used to it.

At times like these, it is vital to slow down, to be quiet, and to take time for reflection; even – and especially – if that is against current practice. For it is sensible to connect with our sources of inner wisdom and to learn to trust the internal compass, our talents, creativity, intuition, and imagination. It is important to know what offers you inner support.

The often-used phrase "standing still is falling behind" shows that we are not really used to focusing our attention inwards. From our earliest school years, we learn to look outwards, to others, rather than inwards. Socialization is largely directed at obedience, performing at the right moment, entering into competition, and maintaining a position in the group. Our main task is to meet the expectations of our parents, teachers, group leaders, and others in authority. We are "out to please" and sensitive to authority. There is little encouragement to think about ourselves, our inner life, and our underlying motives. Before we begin our working lives, we have already been mortally wounded emotionally and spiritually.

Individuals and organizations are, at the moment, on a large scale getting into trouble. Economic miracles from the recent past have turned out to be hypes, and in some cases little more than houses of cards created by bookkeeping tricks. Large-scale fraud has been used to "improve" company figures. This leads to a paralyzing conservatism, because we do not know what other skeletons may jump out of the closet. Even more corporate scandals, or manipulating politicians, made worse by a fear of terrorism – who knows? The result is that frightened premonitions have eroded the trust of the nineties.

Much admired and highly paid managers prove, in a time of disappointing conjuncture, little more than mortals without any supernatural powers. If things are difficult, then all they can apparently do is cut costs and streamline their organization (and in some cases cook the books). Since they are no longer able to manage their complex world, they see little alternative to disciplining their organization. Probably they convince themselves that if their "apparatus" functions better, they will get a better grip on the world. It is the arrogance of impotence.

The "common man" too has become accustomed to riches and success. But as euphoria and prosperity increased, so too has self-criticism and alertness to new developments decreased. In its place is an unctuous feeling of self-importance that makes it increasingly difficult to discuss the basic imperfections of individual or collective actions. Now that push comes to shove, it proves difficult to free ourselves from established behavioral patterns; what's more, we have not really learned to acknowledge our loneliness, imperfection, pain, and sorrow to ourselves and others. If it is "business as usual," then we have to fear more powerlessness, estrangement, exhaustion, and sick leave.

The following quote from the poet Hans Stolp will help us a little along our path: "*Life is like the water of the sea. It washes away until reality remains.*" We must therefore move forward to a world in which a spade is once again a spade. A world in which people accept their responsibility, are prepared to take chances, and, if necessary, to enter into conflict. But that same world is also characterized by care for each other, by team spirit, and commitment to the final result. In other words: today's assignment is to move beyond traditional contradictions and "either/or" thinking. At an individual level, this requires an authentic attitude that is not subservient to the spirit of the times. Only then do we have a solid foundation for conscious self-management and inspirational behavior. Then life will become for us as individuals much more than a voyage of discovery. It will become a process of creation with as the ultimate challenge not only the addition of self-chosen ingredients but also participation in the design of the recipe itself.

A similar theme is found within organizations. In reaction to the countless organizational improvement and revitalization projects, the problems of today are all too frequently approached using the thinking of yesterday and the day before yesterday. The rational analytical approach reigns; we still relate to each other in a highly hierarchical and calculating manner. This archaic work method is at odds with the desired tempo of change and the necessary customer-friendliness. It is also in sharp contrast to the formulated policy that talks about the importance of self-management and entrepreneurial behavior. It is these confusing messages that make people crazy and cynical; they react by throwing in the towel or putting up resistance. It is the cause of many fear-driven patterns: conservatism, egoism, and short-term survival behavior.

It is high time to turn organizations into living and learning organisms. This demands a new level of consciousness that can successfully answer existential and philosophical questions. This, too, requires a new way of thinking – one that leverages the possibilities of today and pro-actively helps to shape these highly interesting times.

Self-determination and self-management on both individual and collective levels is where the future lies. It is essential that the consciousness and behavioral repertoire needed for this are allowed to develop. This is in everybody's interests. On an individual level, the ability to operate from internal strength and actively shape one's own personal or working environment increases. What's more, voluntary and conscious choices activate the feeling of involvement and ownership that can be translated into enthusiastic and responsible working behavior. For organizations, the increase in employee self-awareness and pleasure stimulates a growth in the ability to act pro-actively to changing (market) circumstances.

It is time for real renewal or, as Edgar Schein calls it, "transformational learning." In this process, fundamental suppositions and opinions are subjected to discussion and, where necessary, radically changed. It means that borders are scouted and pushed further. For we can only talk of renewal if those things at the very root of a system or model can be brought into motion. "Renewal" is more than a cosmetic facelift. Thus, the central question in organizational development is probably: who has the courage to undertake change that is fundamental enough.

Since "more of the same" can only lead to greater disaster, the ambition of this book is to promote "renewal." It is all about developing a framework of thinking and experiencing that is suitable to current times. It is a call to finding your own way; authentic and uncompromising, in tune with the spirit of the time and the social environment. But it is also an invitation to develop a true democratic culture around giving work, making work, and receiving work. It is an uncertain adventure, because reality teaches us that the hierarchical and polarized way of thinking has resisted all the storms of the past. The way of thinking proposed by this book will not make the reader's life any easier; it will make it more exciting and genuine.

The book is set up in the following way:

CHAPTER 1: As the title "Twists and Turns" makes clear, this chapter deals with historical leaps in awareness. It describes the necessary evolutions in organizing, managing, and being managed. What clearly emerges is that industrial thinking is *passé* and that we are on the verge of a totally new form of (self) awareness.

CHAPTER 2: Many have become used to a healthy economy that seems to know no end. This has lead many – incorrectly – to attribute the financial success of a company or an individual to their own actions. This chapter, "The Anatomy of the Fib," clearly shows how people often obstruct themselves or fool themselves when it comes to fully expressing their own potential.

CHAPTER 3: Many people feel uneasy with the current speed of change. They feel more or less out of control. The time has come to have the courage to face unpredictability and work with it. This demands a fundamental re-enrichment of the prevalent thinking about self-determination and independence, about excelling and competing. The chapter "Becoming Immune to Dishonesty" clearly shows that it is essential to be honest with yourself. Our choices in life are our own responsibility. Dealing with change in this new era essentially means becoming quieter, being more in tune with your inner theater and concentrating on the Self.

CHAPTER 4: The hierarchal structures of the past are no longer applicable, nor is it appropriate to couple the term "chaos" with the term "catastrophe." Nowadays an organization is run by all those involved. However, in our culture, we still suffer from overestimating or even mythologizing our leaders. Leaders are frequently admired and even worshipped. The chapter "Fallen Heroes" explains that this is no longer relevant. Because it is equally as important that the "followers" exert their influence. Where does real leadership come from in today's changing world?

CHAPTER 5: For years, people believed the dogma that change could be managed. But an organization in which everything is in order is in a state of rigidity. It is time that we learn to forget this control mentality and learn to accept the need for chaos and the associated dynamics of change. (Organizational) change can be identified, but never controlled. In this chapter, the central theme is why change is changing and what management and staff can do to at least avoid getting in the way of forces that want to bring new life to our organizations.

CHAPTER 6: It is advisable to reduce the idea of "organizational change" to more manageable dimensions. Because nothing is more discouraging for action than making the problem greater than what we as humans can take in. For this reason, this chapter gives seven practical tips for "becoming oneself" and surviving in the organizational jungle.

CHAPTER 7: Generally, the author of a management publication is only there as observer and theoretician. This can give rise to the suggestion that he stands above the material and, in that case, leads a totally different life. However, this book about integrity and self-determination, wouldn't be complete without a number of personal observations and motivations.

1

TWISTS AND TURNS

"Life is what happens while you are making other plans."
– John Lennon

WE HAVE SHIFTED from a world with apparently small and understandable risks to one with enormous and unpredictable dangers. Who until recently would have thought it possible that a hi-jacked aircraft would crash on American soil, or that large and trusted companies should, with similar zeal, commit limitless fraud. What is very clear is that trusted reference points have disappeared. For if there is one thing characteristic of current times, then it is the increasing dynamism, instability, and complexity. To understand what is happening today, it is, perhaps, useful to first take a historical perspective. Then it becomes clear that although current trends might fit with previous processes, they are not necessarily a logical consequence. We are dealing here with clear breaks in tradition; in many cases caused by apparently small shifts that have far greater consequences than we could have imagined when they first occurred. A stone thrown in the pond causes long-lasting ripples. A very extreme but failed test-drive in one corner of the world can cause a dent in the image of a world car company and cost hundreds of millions of dollars.

If we are to oversee and keep up with every development, then it is not enough for us to think in terms of purely logical movements and mechanical cause-and-effect reasoning. For example, communications technology is developing at an astounding rate and bringing with it big changes in our way of life. However, predictions made with a linear/digital mindset do not always happen. This is illustrated by the piles of paper in the predicted paperless office. The reality is that there is more paper than ever.

Such fast developments constantly give rise to surprises and stop-and-start changes. We must adapt our consciousness and our attitude to these developments. Because, although everything in the universe is connected, mutually dependent and interactive, our mind often leads us astray into fragmentation and segmentation. We have therefore learned to stop thinking in terms of processes, inter-dependencies, and connections. And we have forgotten that cutting up reality into little pieces is nothing more than a self-created framework that we impose on reality. We create a phantom order because we think this will help us control things. Sometimes that is successful – at least for as long as it lasts. But we must be prepared at all times to change our outlook and to realize that the order is something we have created in our minds and is nothing more than a pragmatic trick.

The way of thinking during the industrial age gave the illusion of understanding and control, but it made the individual less able to make a positive contribution to the greater whole. Today, only those people who have not succumbed to old-fashioned attitudes are able to pro-actively and successfully give shape to the emerging social and organizational reality. That is the greatest challenge for us all.

This chapter is partly inspired by the thinking of Lester Thurow.

EVOLUTION IN TIME AND CONSCIOUSNESS

"Only two things are infinite... The universe and human stupidity."
– Albert Einstein

Changes rarely happen unannounced. They emerge when all circumstances for their appearance have been met. We can talk of a "twist" or "turn" when there is a great leap in the attitude of people toward themselves and toward each other, often accompanied by impressive technological and socio-economic breakthroughs. In Western history, we can identify four specific leaps in consciousness. We will name each period according to its most characteristic feature.

1. *Agricultural era, dominant until around 1800 (tilling the ground, making use of the muscles of man and beast)*
2. *Industrial era, dominant until around 1970 (working with steam, electricity)*
3. *Information era, dominant until around 1990 (working with data)*
4. *Communication era, dominant now (working with information, real time on line).*

The first two industrial revolutions – that of steam approximately 200 years ago and that of electricity approximately 100 years ago – moved masses of people from agricultural to industrial activities.

The agricultural society is relatively transparent. People are part of reasonably closed communities that are dependent on what the land produces. Nature and climate willing, they are quite capable of surviving on their own because they make use of everything suitable in their own environment. The world is made up of small communities that to a high degree are self-sufficient. Society is not disrupted because the electricity breaks down or the price of oil on the world markets sudden soars. That only happens if the harvest "fails," or if there is an outbreak of the plague or war. Religion plays a central role in explaining and gaining acceptance of developments over which people have little control. International trade and politics exist, but still have relatively little influence on the daily lives of the majority of people.

Industrialization heralds in prosperity for a growing population and industrial class. There is an upper layer that is able to develop its knowledge and to specialize. On the other hand, a large and poor industrial proletariat is created that has little more to offer than manual labor. Knowledge is unnecessary and is even considered an obstacle and a threat.

Industrial thinking also changes the relationship between people and their surroundings. For the majority of people, daily contact with and dependence on nature disappears. This is replaced by more prescribed and mechanical relationships. Division of labor makes its appearance. People are placed in large factories to work on small parts of the production process that results in products that roll off the assembly line out of their sight. Tasks are divided and made measurable in tiny time fragments, so that maximum efficiency can be achieved. The bureaucratic organization with its urge for predictability and controllability makes its entrance. In short: people become the means rather than the end, expressed in the rather grim term "the labor factor" (in addition to the capital factor). The demand on human capabilities narrows dramatically. Only much later – in the 1970's – people discover that integrating tasks and using self-directing teams for the production process have a positive effect on quality and work satisfaction.

The third leap into the information era is marked by the arrival of the current knowledge economy which leads people from the industrial sector to the service sector. Mass production as a source of riches, power, and also social contacts is gradually overshadowed by service and an adequate collection and processing of information. A transformation occurs that is just as cataclysmic as the change more than a century ago from the agricultural to industrial era. Those that participate and lead the way do very well. The rest are left not only behind, but a long way behind. The disparity in income has new causes in this era.

The information era of the late 20th century is closely followed by the communication era in the beginning of the 21st century. The time machine is now in overdrive. Communication technology makes working in real time and on line possible. Boundaries became vague. Global capital hangs like a virtual cloud above the earth and can move from one continent to another at a click of the computer. Biotechnology allows us to genetically manipulate everything that lives. Electronic shopping is made possible by Internet and e-mail. Organizations come and go and change their appearance faster than ever. Communication increasingly makes use of cable and satellite technologies. People are therefore forced to rely on themselves and their own individual added value – something that can be measured more accurately than ever – within the work process.

ERA	PACE	SOURCE	DYNAMIC
Communication	>1	Ideas Mindset	Co-creation
Information	>10	Capabilities	Individualization
Industrial	>100	Raw materials	Stand out
Agricultural	>1000	Land	Survival within the group

It is a time of explosive developments in which national borders evaporate, and in which we, partly influenced by information and communication technologies, gradually grow towards a "placeless world" with unknown productive and destructive possibilities. Technology and science can, of course, be used on a large scale for positive results, but also for very hostile results. For this reason, it is desirable that psychological and technological developments go hand in hand with a growth in inner cultivation. A continuing imbalance between these two forces can lead to a loveless application of knowledge and with it irresponsible and egocentric behavior.

Here are some facts that show changes that have taken place during the four eras listed above.

- In the first half of the 19th century, there were about 1 billion people on the earth; now there are 7 billion
- In 1900, people on average lived to the age of 50, now the average is 80 (with women living longer than men)
- In the past, you were old when you reached 40; now this is 70
- In 1900, an eighteen-year-old woman was ready for childbirth; now the average age that women with a university education in a Western country have their first child is 30 (and extends to the age of 40)
- Our forefathers received as much post in their whole lives as we receive in one month
- Products and technologies have an increasingly shorter life cycle.

In this world, characterized by an excess of people, information, and an ever-increasing mountain of changes, traditional thinking about control and external management become more and more problematic. In the traditional industrial and information eras, the functional lines run more or less parallel with the hierarchical lines. Being a boss means being a manager, knowledge center, and information coordinator. In other words: there is something called the "power of the functional position." Fast communication possibilities increasingly erode the foundations for this. People are capable of gathering the required information themselves and gaining authority through this. This is true of relationships in labor organizations.

But it is also true for the consumer, who wants to know precisely where he he can buy a particular product for the cheapest price, and for the patient who confronts his doctor with knowledge and a diagnosis that he has found on the Internet. Organizations are thus required to adopt new ways of thinking about internal management, self-organization, responsibility, and learning and creating together.

ERA	DOMINANT PERCEPTION	CULTURE	COMMUNICATION
Communication	Transformation	Added worth	Inspiration groups
Information	Proactive	Performance	Project meetings
Industrial	Functional	Legitimacy	Office meetings
Agricultural	Adaption	Compliance	Briefings

In the past, it was the collective that defined rules and commandments for the individual. It was an external institute (church or government) that decided what was right and wrong. Internal (self) management was not necessary for society and for those in power at the time it was a hindrance. It was discouraged rather than encouraged. In the area of self-management, we often have the feeling that we have been left empty-handed. This again comes into play now that we are making the transition from a life planned and directed for us to one in which we must give shape to our own future – no longer based on subordination and loyalty, but rather on inner choices and responsibility. In line with these developments, hierarchical-type relationships will (have to) die and be replaced with changing alliances and partnerships, just as, in the past, the ownership of land and resources as a basis for power was replaced by access to knowledge, technology, and good ideas.

TIME MACHINE OUT OF CONTROL

"Our age of anxiety is, in great part, the result of trying to do today's jobs with yesterday's tools." – Marshall McLuhan

At a time when things are accelerating, there is a growing desire for inner peace. It is now vital in the most literal sense of the word to keep "up to date" and to make the best possible use of our own inborn creative powers and flexibility. There is no place for complacency, because every time you think you are there, a new step in the evolution appears or an event occurs which plunges things into even greater chaos. It is all about progressive insight and constant development. As we mentioned earlier, the change does not take place in any logical or "cause-and-effect" way. It is, instead, a chaotic whole made up of numerous impulses. Some are important, others less so, but in the vast majority of cases we can only make the distinction in retrospect. But we *can* learn to remain ourselves in that chaos.

In the period up to and including the information era, our evolution was largely directed at self-realization and progressive individualization. But slowly there arose a desire for combining and connecting and – hopefully – we are now moving in the direction of a society of free, self-directing, communicative, and inspiring people.

ERA	MOTIVE	BEHAVIOR	DESIRE
Communication	Purpose	Interdependent	Inner peace
Information	Self-realization	Independent	Visibility
Industrial	Recognition	Dependent	Acknowledgment
Agricultural	Belonging	Obedient	Material gain

Now that the physical and mental survival for most people is fully taken care of, we have – almost automatically – sufficient space for asking the question: "What makes life worth living?." On an individual level, there are questions such as "How does that help me?" and "What is my contribution?" But collectively there is also the urge to make a contribution to the greater whole. We look critically at whether an activity or relationship is justified. Is it meaningful or meaningless? There is also an increasing desire for the core values of human existence, even and especially in organizations: reliability, respect, responsibility, honesty, care, and community spirit.

	Babyboomers 1946–1960	Generation X 1961–1976	Generatie WHY 1977–
Communication	*Telephone/fax*	*Telephone/e-mail*	*Wireless/mobile*
Leadership	*Feared*	*Requested*	*Tolerated*
Job expectations	*Belonging*	*Pleasure*	*Self-realization*
Change	*Unwanted*	*Unavoidable*	*Desired*
Job opportunities	*Hard to become*	*Talent counts*	*Integration of work and private life*
Justice	*Always wins*	*Usually wins*	*Can be bought*
Instruction	*WHAT*	*HOW*	*WHY*
Technology	*Ignorant*	*Comfortable*	*Adept*

Closer to home and with a narrower time perspective, we can clearly see that at the moment we are experiencing significant change and acceleration processes that remain invisible for many people. What the chart above clearly indicates is just how quickly the developments are taking place and how significant they are. We can talk of accelerating time.

Accelerating time

external management	→	self-management
past and future	→	here and now
possessions + capabilities	→	awareness
rational	→	head and heart
hierarchical thinking	→	co-creation
contracts/ structures	→	internal sense of safety and security
SACRED DUTY	→	DESIRE

The 21st century will once again be sped on by a succession of technologically initiated growth waves. After the ICT growth wave, we expect that biotechnology and nanotechnology – building with atoms – will further influence the development of the consciousness. Each new technology will fuse with the previous one and thus set off a new growth wave. Just as information technology fused with communications technology to become ICT, so ICT will fuse with biotechnology. And after playing around with bits and bytes (information technology) and genes (biotechnology), perhaps we will soon turn our attention to molecules (nanotechnology). They are insidious revolutions, characterized by surprises, setbacks, confusion, and an increasing element of coincidence.

People who now think the new economy is a 'has-been' make the same mistake as those who, at the beginning of the 18th century, thought the industrial revolution was over because a textile factory in Manchester was declared bankrupt. In any case, they deny the existence of a half a billion PCs. That means that, at the moment, there is one computer for every 13 people! They think that internet companies are just a flash in the pan. And they are not connected to the big picture of the various technological developments. For the current digital revolution is but a stage in a much larger and self-accelerating process. It is, in short, a:

DIFFICULT TIME FOR

- *Control freaks*
- *Perfectionists*
- *Rationalists*
- *Planners*
- *Security seekers*

PRACTICAL EXAMPLES OF OUT-DATED THINKING

> *"Self-realization requires responsibility and social awareness. For otherwise there will emerge an overblown self-realization in the shape of self-overestimation, navel contemplation, and egocentricity."*

An important factor that not only causes problems but also keeps them alive is the inability to switch to a consciousness and behavior pattern that is right for today. And we do not even mention here an adequate adaptation of organizations and institutions. We see the results everywhere, but they are particularly visible in politics and corporate life. Politicians get heated about their political primacy, managers about the share price, and employees about their employment guarantees. In the meantime, political parties and trade unions lose members and with them a great part of their legitimacy. Managers lose their credibility with increasing regularity, because they forget that they, too, are employees and choose a one-sided approach for the enrichment of themselves and the shareholders. This is emphasized by the current fashion for share options. They then act not as manager of an organization, but rather as its owner/shareholder.

Similarly, this "more of the same thinking" is apparent on an individual level. For what should we do when material gain bears no direct relationship to a healthy and happy life? Or when the path to success turns out to be a *cul de sac*? People today must almost get into a panic about their own success. And so it is not illogical that many people become slightly depressed around Christmas and ask themselves how they are going to improve their performance even further in the coming year.

We are confronted with questions on all levels that cannot be solved by the well-worn functional and patriarchal thinking. Such as:

- How can we shape our politics within our home borders, while there is an unprecedented internationalization and globalization influenced by economic and technological processes? In many ways, Bill Gates is more influential than George Bush, and George Soros can, with his capital, force the devaluation of sterling. Is there any room in this new world for national or even international decision-making?
- What will be the fate of the credibility of public government? The turnout for elections has, for many years, shown a decline. Voting is no longer automatic, but staying put is. Even though this lacks any legitimacy.
- What will be the fate of political parties and trade unions? The number of members has decreased drastically. Recruiting representatives takes place in an ever-smaller circle. Those people who eventually find themselves in representative roles soon ask themselves what, apart from personal preference, the political influence is on decision-making. And those who are in leadership positions who should be representing their broad constituency at times interpret representation as *selective representation.*
- What will be the fate of that army of formal authorities and their regulatory tasks? It is becoming increasingly clear that developments and transformation take place despite, rather than because

of, those formal authorities. And what about those who fail? If incompetence is revealed, then we seldom ask how it got to this stage. This often means that problem solving becomes some sort of personal redemption ritual and collective learning is thus blocked.

Apparently there is a sense of embarrassment – or is it mental laziness? – when we look at issues such as those mentioned above. In practice, people still, unfortunately, reach for rituals and symbols from some distant past. It is rare that we look for the underlying patterns that caused the problems to arise in the first place. Reducing experience to incidents results in blocking the learning ability. Relying on old ways of thinking is insufficient because institutions and organizational principles from the time of steam and electricity are simply no longer applicable in a timeless and placeless world.

"PICKIN' UP THE PIECES"

"Our organism has a tendency to heal itself, as long as we don't obstruct it with our thought processes." – Charlotte Selver

The "twists and turns" that we have gone through have resulted in a rather fragmented "I." Our role was perfectly clear in the closed agricultural society, but since then we have started to become increasingly diverse components in an increasingly fragmented world. In those parts in which we participate (company, circle of acquaintances, association, church) we use but a limited part of a total behavior pattern and capacities. The environment concerned only requires a limited input.

This is certainly true of the organizations where we work. We are employed to do a certain task that is laid down in a lengthy job description. All the elements in that are carefully weighed against each other and the result is a salary scale, career profile, and so on. But it also determines – although we could say "restricts" – our behavioral repertoire through the environment in which we operate. And because of all these behaviors, a certain corporate culture develops. With much or little room for deviation. And unfortunately we have to admit that in most organizations there is very little room for this indeed.

The reaction is clearly visible: new generations of workers no longer commit themselves one hundred percent to their work, but demand a private life that they keep strictly isolated from their work. But it also becomes clear in other ways that people do not use their capabilities just for their job. Sometimes people choose an easy job, so that they can then use their talents for running an association, playing in a sport club, writing children's books, or in countless other ways. And it is not unusual for such hobbies to develop into "work." There is also a group of people who take their fate into their own hands and start their own company. The most frequently heard reasons are: I get the chance to put my own ideas into practice or: I look at what happens here and think I can do better, and so on.

The one-sided presence of certain competencies and capacities certainly did not arise because people in the organization have only developed in a one-sided way. And a loveless bureaucratic culture did not develop because people in general are incapable of loving collegiality. Distant, authoritarian, and brutal managers can, in their other lives, be loving fathers. Indolent and unmotivated employees can dedicate themselves with heart and soul and with enormous creativity to a sport's club or some ideological society.

But organizations can reduce or even eliminate this division being careful not to neglect the necessary room for diversity. Some large organizations are gradually becoming aware of this by not only employing technicians and economists, but also allowing art historians and philosophers to develop into managers or influential specialists. They realize that an organization can only function in a complex and chaotic society if, internally, there is room for creativity, inter-disciplinary capricious thinking, humor, and – quite often – a degree of chaos.

If we don't do this, then we will simply keep swimming against the tide. And this inevitably results in hopelessness and exhaustion. And we become more and more estranged from the rhythm of time. We literally follow the facts and recognize that "more of the same thinking/acting" only feeds impotence. The associated feeling of displeasure gives rise to primitive reflexes, which causes people to fall even further behind with dated behavior. We can, of course, break this negative spiral, but it demands insight into the inner program of the person involved and faith in his self-healing powers. And sometimes help in discovering and maintaining a good personal path through life.

It is largely a matter of thinking in movement and learning to live with the associated uncertainties. If that happens, then the inborn desire to make a contribution and to achieve a supra-personal meaning will eventually win out. In this original form, people turn out to be – happily – more than just a shell full of molecules and a number of free thoughts and ambitions.

We must take the bull by the horns and change the old way of thinking and behaving. It is time for a new style to emerge, one that embraces initiative, creativity and above all honesty.

2

THE ANATOMY OF THE FIB

"If you are not worth being loved for who you are, then you will have to get admiration for what you can do. Then you will never be abandoned." – Sue Erikson Bloland

For time immemorial, things have been presented as being better than they really are. The truth is often stretched to its limits. Almost nobody is surprised any more when this happens in politics, in advertisements, in management teams, or during negotiations. It is apparently accepted as normal that information is "positioned strategically," that we conceal certain facts, and that we don't tell the whole story. We expect our opponent to feed us misinformation and play politics, and we even anticipate it; and our opponent expects the same from us. In many companies, those who master the mechanics of the fib make the most brilliant careers. One of the first things you learn in your career is that you must never, ever confront your boss – and certainly never in public – with uncomfortable information.

Just how common fabrication is and how necessary it is to anticipate it is shown in the following example. A bank that lends money has to be aware that companies have a tendency to conceal their weak spots. Bankers are often judged on the new loans they arrange and that often means that regulations are not applied with due strictness.

Our language has many expressions for masking or even justifying such untruths: "What he doesn't know won't hurt him," "A little white lie," and so on. Fibbing or "stretching the truth" is not only about throwing sand in the opponent's eye, but also about deceiving ourselves. In such a situation, it is not easy to trust our inner compass or even find it. Not being totally honest begins in our early childhood, where striving for "happy peace" soon turns into the "fear of harmony." When we have already learned to live with emotional price-performance analyses, we enter our first school years where we learn to look outwards rather than inwards. It is all about gathering factual knowledge and solving practical problems that exist around us. We are not encouraged to think about ourselves, our inner life, or our motives. Those who do well at school have basically learned to jump through the hoops that others hold up for them. This earns applause and even a degree of freedom; but it seldom develops trust in our inner knowledge and our own intuition.

Once we end up in corporate life, the conditioning of obedience and creating good headlines continues. We learn in this context – and possibly even through courses in social skills – to improve our presentation and lecturing techniques, or to become more customer-friendly or more collegial. Without an appropriate inner foundation, such courses end up compounding artificiality. People are literally made more artificial. These are forms of brainwashing, which only widens the gap between what we feel inside and what we pretend to be to the outside world. Things can go well for a time until the gap reveals itself under the pressure to perform. Then the proud castle is suddenly found to rest on a cardboard foundation.

Of course there will always be a degree of tension between wish and reality and between strength and burden. Perhaps we exist thanks to the tension between what we are deep inside and what we pretend to be. For deeply happy people rarely have a longing to change and without inner unrest, few people would grow into a more complete state of "being." What we want to achieve is the ability to bridge the gap between what we are inside and what we pretend to be to the outside world. This will allow for individual development and self-awareness.

> *"Really loving somebody is all about wanting to feel and being able to feel; it is about understanding what the other wants and needs and then helping them fulfill these needs."* – Ingeborg Bosch

It begins early. Although parents normally love their children and would like to understand the wants and needs of their children and fulfill them, it does not always work out that way. It is not intentional, but parents can only give what they have developed in themselves and have available for somebody else. The child often has to find its own way, which isn't easy even for a highly intelligent child. Children with an above-average (emotional) aptitude have an above-average vulnerability. In her book *The Drama of the Gifted Child*, Alice Miller writes: "The drama of the intelligent and perceptive child is that it recognizes at an early age the aspirations of its parents and adapts to them."

With this "ideal self," that exists largely in the subconscious, a child tries to deal with the high expectations in its surroundings. The inner message reads: to be accepted and to be worth anything, it is necessary that I fit the image I have created or imposed on myself. If I am to consider myself of any value, I must then satisfy this "ideal self." With mechanical regularity, the child tells itself and others what it *must* think, feel, and do, and that it must be *perfect*. There may be nothing left of any real self-acceptance or forgiveness.

Using this pattern of behavior, the child learns to automatically suppress its innermost but "forbidden" feelings, and thus develops insufficient trust in the integrity of its own feelings. This increases the pressure on its trust in its surroundings, and the result is fear. This is unpleasant and then follows the (largely implicit) decision to avoid the (imagined) pressure from the surroundings. The escape routes present themselves:*

* This model is inspired by the Past Reality Integration Therapy thinking of Ingeborg Bosch.

- *False hope* The child tries even harder to do its best in the (false) hope that by doing this its emotional needs will one day be fulfilled. The child says to itself: "If I really do my best, then they will eventually come to love me more." In this way, the feeling of one's own value becomes inextricably linked with performance and prestige. In adulthood, this conditional self-acceptance is frequently the source of perfectionism and an unbridled urge to prove oneself. For the perfectionist, it is rarely "good enough."
- *False power* The child convinces itself that its emotional needs do not need to be fulfilled by its surroundings. The child says when confronted with painful situations: "I can handle it," or "That doesn't bother me" or "I don't have a problem, you just see things incorrectly." In adulthood, this leads to a pattern of exaggerated self-sufficiency ("Nothing can hurt me") and/or an assertive need for control ("As long as I am in charge, nothing can happen to me.").
- *False modesty* The child blames itself for the fact that its emotional needs are not fulfilled. The child apologizes for its surroundings: "I didn't receive any attention, because I was a stupid child," or "It is all my fault, because I never dared object." In adulthood, this frequently leads to a pattern of false modesty ("If I was really any good, I would not be working here") and to an exaggerated timidity to choose a clear position in situations of tension ("I'm careful about saying what I really think").

For the child, these are initially survival or defensive mechanisms that protect it against the big bad world – even if the world isn't that bad after all. Nobody raising a child is able to fulfill every single need that child may have for attention, safety, support, and warmth. And so it is inevitable that each of us starts life with a certain sense of emotional confusion. If the underlying fears are not confronted, these will create permanent mechanisms; even when, as an adult, such lines of defense are no longer needed.

The status quo feels safe; a pattern has emerged that helps the child exist in what feels like an unsafe world. Every new experience is translated into the language of this established behavioral pattern. The intrusion of other thoughts and feelings causes fear, because they can upset the existing equilibrium. Everything seems to be in order – but it is nothing more than a cardboard castle. The fear grows as the distance between the outer and inner worlds increases. Once they have arrived at this point, most people have little desire to "open old wounds." These old wounds are too stark a reminder of feelings of misunderstanding, helplessness, and loneliness.

The vicious circle that has emerged looks like this:

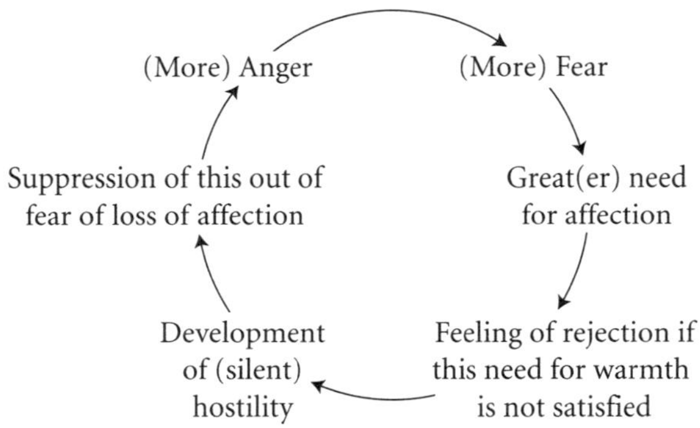

The unhealed pain causes us to constantly get in our own way. It doesn't help that the outside world then becomes less inclined to answer the implicit cry with warmth and attention. The more people clamp onto the ideal-self, the more difficult it becomes for them to create a happy self-image and to allow themselves to act according to their true feelings. Ultimately, a larger gap forms between the ideal self and the real self, with disastrous results for the authenticity and self-confidence of the individual.

In order to bridge this gap and improve one's self-image, we should confront our own fears, move past our childhood experiences and patterns, and accept ourselves for who we really are.

EGOCENTRICITY

> *"We are not held in the iron grasp of the past, but in the iron grasp of the illusion that we have to protect ourselves from what happened to us in the past. When we relive what really happened, then today is generally surprisingly unencumbered."* – Ingeborg Bosch

People are frequently concerned about themselves: "What are the consequences for me?," "Will I survive?," and "Can I really handle it all?" In other words: the primary perspective is whether a possible change could serve one's own interests. Now there is nothing wrong with healthy self-interest. But it is something else when fear gains the upper hand over trust, curiosity, and creativity. In other words, when fear and self-interest win over love and attachment, the result is an egocentric survival behavior that characterizes and paralyzes both people and organizations. Here, everybody has his or her self-interest in mind, with no regard for the consequences for the group or society. Alas, this phenomenon is all too common in change processes. Then we meet the "disfigured ego" in its most primary guises:

- Arrogance
- Authoritarian and corporate political behavior
- Fear
- Doubt.

These are expressions of fear and insecurity that, certainly when combined, cause confusion and exhaustion. If this is actually taking place and we feel chronically unwell, then there are only two ways out: suppress the people in your surroundings or suppress yourself. The result of either strategy is the same. Change activities are robbed of their vitality and credibility. Any approach toward renewal must address the disfigured ego.

MASKS

"Between the public and non-public world, there is often a mask of fear."

No relationship can exist without sufficient care and love for the whole. It is therefore necessary that people be prepared to put their self-interest into context and to rise above it if the interests of the group demand that. When this doesn't succeed sufficiently and when exploitive behavior wins over solidarity, then every relationship/group finds itself in trouble. Highly personal survival behavior emerges aimed at maintaining the *status quo*. The question of whether everybody is happy with this has long lost any importance. The law for maintaining misery comes into force. The disfigured ego is caught up in fear and does everything possible to remain in control; even if that only gives an appearance of control. Ultimately everybody loses. Fear is in command and there is a deathly silence around relationships. If things cannot be pulled together, then the only thing that remains is to clamp onto the existing image of reality. This clamp becomes more severe if people feel they are successful and materially prosperous. The conclusion is reached all too quickly: "He's doing a good job." Worse: success is often attributed to the problematical behavior.

What other people think of all this doesn't matter in the least: "You've got it all wrong, after all I'm a success." Once this state of mind has been reached, then the ego is best served with distance and disagreement. Without this distance, somebody could come up with the idea of bursting his bubble. The psychological motto is: "Don't come too close or I'll eliminate you before you become too big a risk." The following lines of defense have one thing in common, they both make sure reality doesn't intrude. We take a look at some of the expressions (masks) that are adopted by the disfigured ego:

The Know it-all reasons from his own assumptions and enjoys entering into a debate with the objective being to polarize things. He wants to win and prove that he is the strongest.

The Ego-tripper is only interested in himself with the central theme: How do I get the most out of the situation? Masters every story and turns everything towards himself.

The Boaster compensates a fragile self-image by making out reality as better than it is. The boaster is constantly living above his station and presents himself as better than the rest.

The Joker uses humor as a shield against the outside world. He constantly puts everything into perspective and the "humor" is often at the expense of somebody else.

The Opportunist wants to exert influence, without being guided and/or hindered by underlying principles, values, and norms. The ruling thought here is: How do I save myself from this.

The Big Shot always wants to be the biggest, the best, the first, the cleverest, the fastest; in any case better than his brother, his neighbor, or his colleague.

The Control Freak wants leadership and control, to hold the reigns. The ruling thought is: "Trust is good, control is better."

The Divider sets people against each other and exists thanks to disagreement. The divider does not direct things in public, but prefers to operate from the back room.

The Squirmer sets one truth next to another without choosing for either. In this way, maximum freedom is created.

The Political Animal is infatuated with changing coalitions and force fields. He adores hidden agendas and unpaid bills.

The Denier has never done it, is innocence in the flesh; how can anybody ever doubt this (attack is the best form of defense).

The Difficulty Seeker can never believe that anything is simple, because that's boring. In order to stay out of the firing line, the difficulty seeker is best served by complicated reasoning and contradictions. He is determined to make things unnecessarily complicated.

The Ostrich cannot live with reality because the gap between fact and fiction is too large. He avoids responsibility. Denial and loss of memory are the best escape routes.

The Victim explains current behavior by continuously pointing a finger at circumstances and incidents about which he could do nothing. The fault is always somebody else's (external attribution).

The Martyr exhibits behavior that has the character of unselfishness, although the underlying desires and needs are never made explicit. The central theme here is: How to I stay out of the firing line? This is one of the most advanced forms of egocentricity.

The problem with these masks is that they cause a double relationship to develop with the person's mirror image. The person may like to think they are the best-looking boy or girl in the class, but deep down they know this is not really the case. They are scared the mirror will break. They say that they would really like to change and seem to seriously desire inner peace. They can even be jealous of people who have achieved this. But for any change on the level of "being" to take place, the mask must be shed and the all important step cannot be missed: *self-acceptance.*

RUNNING AWAY FROM SHAME, PAIN, AND SORROW

> *"What lies behind us, and what lies before us are tiny matters compared with what lies within us."* – Ralph Waldo Emerson

In our search for the sources of dishonesty we quickly come up against the inability of modern man to deal with adversity. Now of course it is perfectly natural to want to avoid pain and to seek pleasure. But it is not a good idea to pretend that we live in Disneyland and that life is just one big bowl of cherries. Hard times must be expected and accepted too. A person gains character during moments of adversity or pain. Therefore, it is sensible to develop our inborn resistance to deal with such moments.

Over the years, many of us have grown quite accustomed to success and prosperity. We have become a "good weather society:" where almost everybody is "happy and healthy" and everything comes up roses. Anything that isn't perfect must be urgently repaired, if necessary using cosmetic surgery, public relations, and carefully corrected financial data. In any case, many people experience a strong social pressure to mask the imperfect or at least keep it to themselves. "If it isn't good news, then I don't want to hear it." In such a social climate, it can be difficult to have integrity and remain true to yourself and even more so if life becomes painful or you find yourself feeling isolated. Nobody is really waiting for your doubts, insecurity, or sorrow. And so, early on, we learn to choose the beautiful illusion above emotional reality and we think our image is more important than sincere communication about what is really taking place deep inside. People start living in two worlds. Emotions are hidden behind masks of hypocrisy and pain is denied or at least kept far out of sight. We start playing a role in film and décor of our own making. The script's main characters are: fear and its little brother, guilt. It looks like life, but it isn't real. We live a split life with different realities and carefully practice our ability to play the chameleon. And then we are left alone with just one question: How on earth can we play the hero in our own film?

This exaggerated concern for what the outside world thinks of us has disastrous side effects for the development of our emotional life. Many people have become so masterful at suppressing their emotions that they have lost contact with the feelings that take place deep inside. A wise man once said, "When man invented the mirror, he lost contact with his soul." What can you do if you don't feel as "happy and healthy" as the rest of the world suggests you should be. What do you do if you are confronted with serious questions about life or with illness or death processes? What do you do if your need for support and comradeship is not satisfied, because you have taught yourself not to ask for them?

In times of need it becomes very clear how we previously dealt with ourselves and others. If we had the habit of keeping people at arm's length, always giving the impression that we were self-sufficient, and invested very little into relationships, it can be difficult to ask others for help and to appeal to the generosity of friends and colleagues. It becomes increasingly difficult to admit our vulnerability and to place our fate in the hands of others. Thus the feeling of loneliness only increases and many, often unarticulated fears begin to play an ever-greater role. It becomes increasingly difficult to look at the situation honestly. We can feel a deep need for contact but at the same time do not know how to handle this. Perhaps the biggest obstacle here is understanding that our emotional bank account with those around us is deep in the red. If you don't give, you don't get. What's more, there is so much fear of touching our accumulated pain and accompanying sorrow that we start projecting like mad. These projections quickly assume the character of judgments and disqualifications of others. That is why deeply scared people have such a need to make comments about other people or to pass judgment on them. So the pain manifests itself in value judgments about others. And pain-laden patterns repeat themselves, even from one generation to the next. The explanation is simple: everything you don't clear up will lie at your feet (or at the feet of your children).

That is why it is vital to develop a natural attitude towards the imperfect, unpleasant, and sometimes painful part of our existence. Because pain and sorrow are just like bad weather. Everybody hates it, but it returns with a certain regularity. There is no use getting angry at bad weather; you can, perhaps, better assume that it might rain. What's more, living with a little misfortune is exactly the art of life. And thus there is nothing wrong with authentic emotions such as fear, sorrow, and anger, even though they might cause some temporary anguish. What is certainly bad is suppressing these forces. These then turn into aggression and result in harm to yourself or damage to others. It is therefore important to learn to recognize these emotions and to understand where they come from. Anger often has a relationship with accumulated sorrow from the past and fear of the future is explained by the memory of this pain. As long as fear determines our thinking, then the chance is great that old painful experiences will keep repeating themselves. Sorrow and anger by themselves are not the evil-doers. The painful power of these emotions rests in how they are handled. Trying to suppress these feelings rarely makes them go away and often has the reverse effect of making these feelings last longer. There is nothing against pain, there is everything against suppressed pain.

NATURAL EMOTIONS	DISFIGURED EMOTIONS
Sorrow	Chronic depression
Anger	Rage
Fear	Panic
Envy	Jealousy
Love	Possessiveness

If handled in the right way, all the accumulated pain, anger, and sorrow can, fortunately, be transformed into strength. But you must be prepared to see what is actually happening, to live in the here and now, and learn to talk. For little has such a healing effect as being in deep contact with somebody else. And nothing creates a better connection than looking into the uncertain inner world of somebody else. What's more, mutual communication about emotions helps each recognize their own discomfort. For how can you sympathize with the suffering of another if you have no idea of what suffering is?

From this perspective, we can state that dishonesty is not a result of a congenital falsehood or moral inability, but rather the lack of courage to get into deep contact with ourselves or others. We neglect or forget to develop fully the inborn ability for self-definition and self-determination. We suppress our emotions. Or put more simply: we need to put our trust in what is really ours – our feelings and our intuition.

NOTHING FAILS LIKE SUCCESS

"Try not to become a man of success, but rather try to become a man of value." – Albert Einstein

Until just recently we have had, with just a few interruptions, a continuous growth in company turnover and profit. With the growing euphoria and welfare, there is often a decline in self-criticism and alertness to new developments. Their place has been taken by a balmy feeling of self-satisfaction that makes it increasingly difficult to talk about essential imperfections in individual and collective functioning. Thus, people could believe – or their existing belief could become stronger – that their success and the success of their company bore a direct relationship to the quality of the way they functioned. A miscalculation that is proving destructive. A mental laziness grew that, in combination with self-satisfaction, made us lose our fighting spirit. And we have become insensitive or even resistant to minor warning signals.

NOTHING FAILS LIKE SUCCESS

- *Self-Satisfaction/conceit*
- *Lazyness*
- *Introversion*
- *Apathy*

The reality, however, becomes clear when times are economically more difficult. Now the economy is on the decline so we start to see the difference between organized success and cheaply achieved success. In other words: the difference is highlighted between people and companies that really do well and people and companies who have simply profited from the general prosperity.

Now that things come down to performance and the added value of the individual and the organization, it seems impossible for us to free ourselves from established patterns of behavior. Because we have not really learned to live with solitude, imperfection, pain, and sorrow.

MORE SOURCES OF ALIENATION

"Pain is unavoidable, suffering is a choice." – Jagdish Parikh

Our western view of the world is based on a strict separation of heaven and earth, rationality and emotion, coincidence and calculation, policy and execution, management and employees, ethics and economy, work and pleasure.

SEPARATIONS

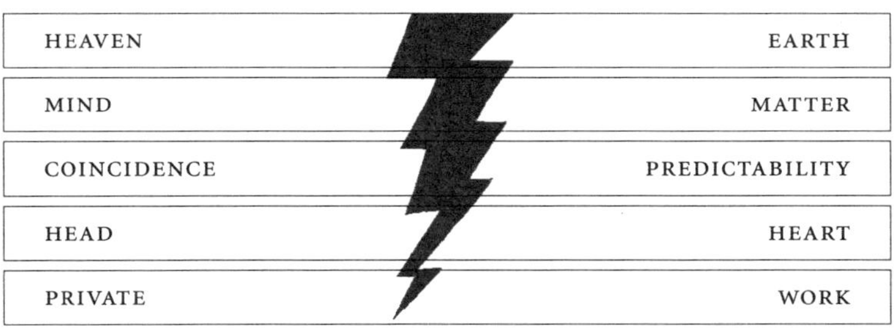

And so we have forgotten to think in a totality. The associations have been lost. Because of this development and the connected over-accentuation of analytical purity, there is little chance for our

inborn abilities for admiration, intuitive decision-making, and creative thinking. This has all sorts of consequences:

- In the grown up world , it is no longer sufficient to trust and follow your feelings. The often implicit demand made of communication processes is that you must be able to support everything with arguments.
- For many, earning money (filling) and giving content to life (fulfilling) have become two completely separate issues.
- There is pressure to express cultural progress in measurable units. We have become blind to processes that cannot be immediately expressed in "shareholder value" or "return on investment."
- The growing insecurity about physical and human processes leads to alienation, exhaustion, and negative stress. Until the body ultimately brings out its veto.

We have suppressed the human measure and an increasing amount of energy is used in fear-directed survival patterns: conservatism, egocentricity, and opportunism. Intuition, spontaneity and raw honesty have suffered as a result.

Fortunately, our deep rooted human nature is not easily dismissed. Our whole being will resist such a snub, if necessary with self-destruction. For just as a life centered around an inner core leads to clarity and meaning, so one without inner direction will result in division and a sense of meaninglessness.

SEPARATIONS

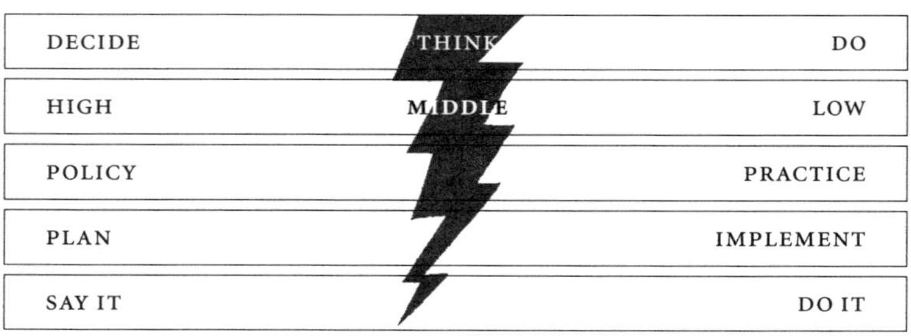

In organizations too there is a strict division between making policy and executing policy. This often means that thinkers are far removed from practice, and practical people will make sure they don't think. What has been put asunder must once again be united. Not in the old way, but in a new and meaningful way. This desire is universal and explains the interest around us in emotional and spiritual intelligence.

THE GAP BETWEEN POLICY AND EXECUTION

> *"Modern organized artificiality cannot be rhymed with inner simplicity. Where the two clash, you will always find flagrant self-deceit or rude hypocrisy."* – Ghandi

With so many people alienated from their core, it is hardly surprising that organizations, too, are losing touch with their essential self. In fact, it is difficult to find any social area where policy and execution have so little to do with each other as in organizations. That is, by the way, true of both profit and non-profit organizations. The extent of the alienation generally increases, as scale gets larger. Until what (once) was agreed has nothing whatsoever to do with what actually takes place. A few examples of this duality:

- Despite all the writings about modern and human-oriented management, things within organizations have become harder and more exploitive. The rational, bookkeeping approach dominates and relationships are still essentially hierarchical and functional. Apparently the concepts of vision-directed actions and self-management have been rationally developed but have still not been emotionally embraced or experienced by sufficient numbers of people. Consultants and management trainers often run ahead of reality.
- Despite the often excessive policy concerning personnel assessment and career development, the reality within many organizations is that management decisions are taken opportunistically and

people try to protect each other. Lengthy trainings about discussion techniques and personnel assessment have too seldom contributed to the emergence of transparent relationships and realistic assessments. While this remains the case, underlying rituals in practice will frequently contribute to the emergence of untruthful work relationships.

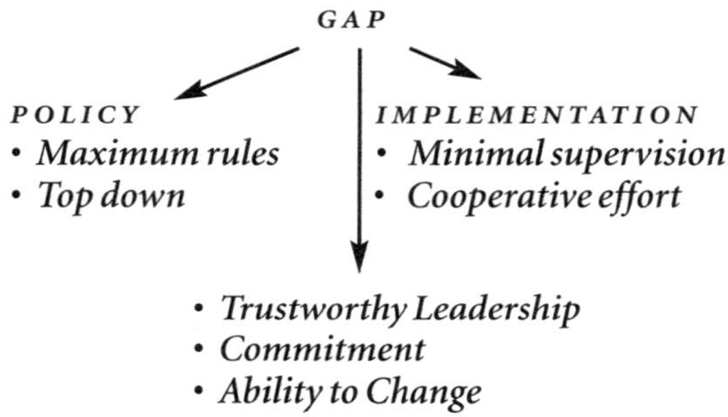

This context, together with the increasing pressure to perform and the excessive consumption, can be enormously alienating. Many try to keep up with the Joneses and embrace the dominant culture in their surroundings. If necessary, they are even prepared to damage themselves and adopt comfortable norms and values that do not match their own convictions.

Thus there is an ever-greater gap between what is pretended and what is realized; between must and want, between feeling and rationality. Creating new or additional policy is, in many organizations, more popular than the hard work needed to implement the current policy. What's more, people concentrate on policy that improves manageability, without paying sufficient attention to the content and process dimensions.

In the visual triangle formed by management (meaning), control (predictability) and climate (atmosphere, motivation), people seem to err towards exertions that aim to make the organization more controllable. The red-tape mechanism then replaces other regulatory mechanisms such as alignment of mission and vision and a shared feeling of do's and don'ts (culture). When this happens, then a remarkable and impoverished game takes place. The top tries to remain in control by exerting as much force as possible. Subordinates try to avoid things with as much creativity as possible.

And so the result is a situation in which policy and execution have less and less to do with each other and employees have the feeling that they must "make the best of things." Frequently, this development turns into a silent war between policy-makers and people who execute the policy, and an increasing amount of creativity is pumped into finding ways to "get round" the rules. Until nobody considers himself responsible for the current situation or even has a hope that it will ever change for the better. This role-play then reaches its impertinent perfection: everybody acts as if they really care about the system, but at the same time "do their own thing" in silence.

SELF-DENIAL AND SELF-BETRAYAL

> *"The unfortunate thing about this world is that good habits are so much easier to give up than bad ones."* – Somerset Maugham

Once you've started to live with your own definition of the truth, it's not easy to give it up. In the book *Leadership and Self-Deception*, the Arbinger Institute clarifies the dynamic and self-reinforcing character of inner alienation. The core of this argument is that by not following your feeling and intuition, you are forced into an ever-tighter corner with less room to maneuver. The further you go, the harder it becomes to deviate from the chosen path and to admit to yourself and others that you are on the wrong road. In this way, you are not the only one who gets into a fix, but also those around you. Essentially, this is what happens:

1 A situation demands that you make a choice
2 This choice you make follows your feelings/intuition or is diametrically opposed to them
3 You have the inclination to justify the choice
4 You begin to filter information and see the world in a way that justifies your choice
5 Characteristic patterns emerge for you and those around you for dealing with the ramifications of the choice.

It is not advisable to make choices that are at odds with your feelings. For then, before you realize it, selective perception and self-denial will take the place of being true to yourself and having open contact with those around you. That is probably why the Arbinger Institute uses the severe term "self-betrayal" for this behavior.

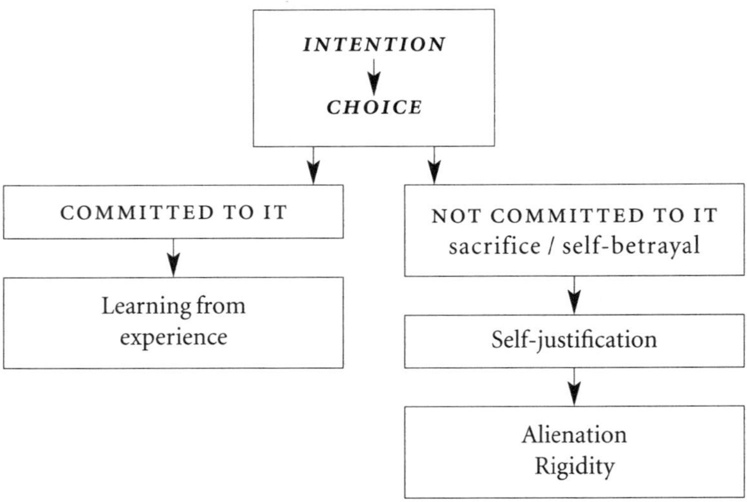

SELF-JUSTIFICATION CONSTRUCTIONS

"Fame is not an effective remedy for feelings of inadequacy."
– Sue Erikson Bloland

When the gap between our feelings/intuition and our behavior widens, then we need more self-justification. There is, after all, a lot more that we have to explain to ourselves, even if we feel the final choice cannot really be explained. As time passes, certain ways of thinking become characteristic for the way we stand in our lives. They become cast-iron constructions that are used to justify the idea that it is not always possible or desirable to follow your feelings. And so many people simply decide to "stay put" with their employer or partner. Because the grass isn't greener anywhere else. Or perhaps they cherish the expectation that freedom will come when they get their pension. And so they distance themselves gradually from any inner desire they might have had for a more passionate life and the accompanying silent desperation is simply accepted. Their fear has taken hold.

Self-justification constructions are artificial interventions by the brain designed to lull people to sleep. By accepting them completely, we can keep on doing what we've always done and won't need to take action. The following eight constructions are frequently used:

1 *Unmotivated belief in progress* Instead of placing clear consequences on perceived unhappiness, we hope that the unhappiness will soon disappear through a change in the situation. "We'll get a new boss or the economy will improve."
2 *Solidified cynicism* Simply assume that the situation elsewhere is no better. Why go to all the trouble of changing places when "it's all the same wherever you go"?
3 *Idealized egocentricity* If the whole is going badly, then it is obvious that you have to concentrate exclusively on your own area of responsibility. Then you can, with a degree of pride, explain that things are going exceptionally well in your section.

SELF-JUSTIFICATION CONSTRUCTIONS

1	UNFOUNDED EXPECTATIONS *(it'll be better soon)*
2	CYNICISM *(there's always something wrong)*
3	IDEALIZED EGOCENTRICITY *(I focus on my own affairs)*
4	FEIGNED LOYALTY *(I can't let my people down)*
5	PARALYZING COMPLEXITY *(it can't be this simple)*
6	MAGNIFIED VULNERABILITY *(let's just keep the peace)*
7	LIMITED PERSONAL ENJOYMENT *(it's not what I always dreamed of but it's fine)*
8	PATTERN DENIAL *(this was an isolated incident)*

4 *Feigned loyalty* This construction also has, as its basis, a way of looking at your own importance through rose-colored glasses. "The organization may be functioning badly, but I can't abandon my people."

5 *Paralyzing complexity* Many people seem to think it important to make the situation more complex. In this way, they mask their lack of courage to take the consequences for their feelings of displeasure. "It really can't be as simple as all that."

6 *Exaggerated vulnerability* A lot of "think what you like but never say it" behavior can be explained by the frequent assumption that existing relationships are too fragile to strain them with one's emotional reality. "We have such a good time here."

7 *Lowered level of ambition* If everything seems to be going

wrong, then the easiest conclusion is that it can't be as bad as all that. Certainly not compared to people who are in a worse situation. "It may not be perfect here, but at least it's tolerable." In this context, people who go for gold are inveterate optimists.

8 *Denial patterns* One of the most advanced forms of self-denial is to couple feelings of unease to the fact that problems only occur incidentally. In this way, the problem is given less weight and you create for yourself a justification for not dwelling on the feeling of unease that has already arisen.

The scenarios listed above show clearly how people try to convince themselves and those around them that their inaction is justified. They are psychologically logical reactions to situations of increased pressure. The behavior is, of course, in some ways rewarded. Avoiding the confrontation or denying the problem may result in short-term stress reduction. And yet it is important not to pull the wool over their eyes. Because everything you leave lying around will be there to stumble over.

THE LANGUAGE OF DECEPTION

"A large lower class has emerged; not poor by material standards, but poor in self-respect." – Marcel van Dam

A characteristic of deception is that only a few people admit to it in public. Certainly, if one is aware of his own deceptive behavior, then it is perhaps better to keep it a private matter. We can thus assume that a lot of energy is put into hiding unspoken deliberations.

And yet a good observer can track down the nature of somebody's inner choice processes. You only need to listen to the language being used by your conversation partner and be aware of the conviction and credibility of his or her words. The current language of organizations, however, does not make things easier. A German linguist,

Uwe Pörksen used the description "Plastikwörter" (empty words) when attending a congress about technology, he noted that speaker after speaker talked about "progress," "modernization," "development," "necessity," "communication," "information," "crisis," "management." One of the guests suggested that the congress could be condensed into just one hundred words, to which another answered: "One hundred? Fifty at the most!" It is very easy to hide behind impressive words and pretend that you are one of the in-crowd.

Equally recognizable is the terminology we use to package our non-commitment. Many people and companies suffer from the "say yes but mean no" virus. This frequently occurs when people feel obliged to do something in which they have little or no belief. In order to avoid an open confrontation with the people at the top, they agree to co-operate; but then without too much inner commitment. You can almost hear them thinking: "We'll try and just hope that we succeed." Or "in itself and in principle" it's a good suggestion. Or people move into the corridors and explain that the management may want them to do it, but it'll never work. Communicating in such an environment means skirting the issue as closely as possible and is aimed particularly at ensuring that you can never be held responsible for a possible failure.

POLITICAL LANGUAGE
Provokes doubt/irritation
Uses "doublespeak"
Loses attention
Bores and alienates
Invites debate

Authentic language has a different sound and emotional meaning to it. You can hear that the speaker is talking from the heart and that he or she really means it. Yes means yes, and a promise is more than a vague, and not really committed, intention to act. The use of language is clear and transparent and leaves nothing to the imagination. The number of words is often limited. You have the impression that you are really talking to somebody.

AUTHENTIC LANGUAGE
Is expressive
Is inescapable
Touches/moves
Deepens the contact
Invites dialog

Fortunately, not everybody fits into a world in which "glorious illusion" takes the place of sincere communication. What's more, it regularly becomes clear that the need for a (limited) number of trustworthy confidants is universal. And what is such a relationship other than one in which you can simply be yourself? And in which you can, without gilding the lily, talk about things that are really important to you.

BOSS FEAR

> *"Relationships cannot flourish if they are clamped onto a background of suppression."*

One of the most primitive life forms on earth is the master/servant relationship. Although trust in each other's intentions lies at the root of every healthy exchange of ideas, in many companies the fear of what one can do to the other has the upper hand. While this fear dominates the consciousness, there will be a lot of manipulation of information. After all, you can spice things up or leave them unsaid. As a result, more and more decisions will be taken based on inaccurate or incomplete information. In addition, people will become increasingly careful – or look for salvation elsewhere.

In their book *The Knowing-Doing Gap*, Jeffrey Pfeffer and Robert Sutton suggest that knowledge itself is not of vital importance in creating a competitive advantage but rather the way it is put to use. Relevant knowledge is accessible to virtually everybody, but very few companies are able to bridge the gap between knowing and doing. Boss Fear is, according to them, the most important reason for the gap.

Boss Fear has at least two sides:

- *Employees fear bosses* On a large scale, people consider and anticipate the expectations – whether actually articulated or not – of those next to the highest bosses. People eagerly say what the boss wants to hear; either to get into the boss's good books or to avoid the boss's antipathy. This last one in particular can result in considerable individual discomfort. People sometimes decide to essentially exchange their freedom for the hope of a better future and the possibility of promotion. And we give away our right of self-determination to those who, in exchange for this, are expected to protect us. The bottom line is an implicit psychological deal: subjection in exchange for safety. In the animal world, this behavior has a clear function; it can be observed in many species, including primates. But for humans who want to rise above this level, this deal – certainly in the long term – can have disastrous consequences for self-respect and the feeling of individual value. For a company, it can lead to the destruction of knowledge and increasing difficulty in timely renewal.
- *Bosses fear employees* Where there is fear there can be no love. And thus managers suffer from the fear-generated actions of their employees. The argument here is not only about the selective and rose-colored information that is given. But also it must be immense-

ly troubling for the human being in the manager to be seen as nothing more than a role model and always treated with reserve. Because, in that role, you are expected to be a man of steel, to set the good example, to know all the ins and outs, and never to have a weak moment. This is much too heavy a load and source of fear of failure and paralysis: it is inevitable that they can never meet such expectations. Most managers keep this fear to themselves and make sure they never reveal it. There are too many people waiting and hoping for their downfall.

If, within a relationship, it becomes unsafe for one partner, then it is unsafe for both. Boss and employee both profit from an optimal relationship, even if it is only to give humanity a chance. But business performance, too, gains from an optimal exchange of information. Sharing knowledge means multiplying knowledge. That is only possible in healthy and open work relationships. If managers want to achieve results at any cost, then this will lead to a raw survival mode and can invite falsification of information. And since "stress causes stupidity," the learning ability of the collective is also damaged. This makes it increasingly difficult and time consuming to realize real renewal, and can undermine the successful ability of the company.

THE ORGANIZATION AS THE HOUSE WHERE NOBODY WANTS TO LIVE

> *"Most CEOs are in manic defence; they are constantly on the run, because if they stand still they will be asked exactly what they are running for."* – Manfred Kets de Vries

In many organizations, there is a lot of accumulated suffering. It doesn't take much to conjure up negative experiences. It is often about deeply felt disappointment and sorrow. If they are to be dealt with, then words must be given to them; new energy can only arise if blockages are recognized and discussed.

Of course there are positive sounds – but generally later in the contact. People aren't born with negativity. They want nothing better than that things go well for the company. A human heart is, after all, more than a pump, an organization more than a machine.

Attempts to keep processes rational and controllable often waver dangerously on emotional currents that do not match the rational world above. It is like spiders caught in their own webs, because nobody wants to lose comforting habits – even though such habits are deadly for the vitality of the organization, for the credibility of people, and for the self-value of the individual. Such a bureaucracy creating behavioral system produces incidents, delays, and a dishonest mentality, no matter who is in the cast. More of the same approach leads predictably to more incidents, more delays, and more dishonesty. In this climate, a salary is exchanged as barter for sacrifices in work enjoyment and creativity.

This situation is made tolerable by an empty promise of progress. People continue to function within organizations because this is their ticket to financial gain, status, and social security. For this they are prepared to sacrifice their deeper, personal desires. Achieving efficiency and economic growth is more important than anything else, more important, even, than personal well-being, society, and the environment. One question is avoided: what are all these efforts good for? It is any wonder that people ultimately react to this with instinctive negativity? People who are intelligent, who like to think and decide for themselves, deserve more space. Otherwise they will leave or give up, because nobody has studied to become a robot.

3

BECOMING IMMUNE TO DISHONESTY

> *"I live two lives each day*
> *One the way I must and one my own way.*
> *Oh when will I find it again in my heart*
> *To live my life the way before it grew apart."*
> – Guillaume van der Graft

THE POST-WAR Western society has disintegrated from a reasonably stable organism into a society in which egotism, consumption, and individualism have become the most important stimuli. This focus on individualism and short-term gain has increased the emphasis on self-interest. The neighbor can look after the collective; but the neighbor thinks the same. We no longer consider norms binding; we think that, as individuals, we are quite entitled to ignore a norm that we feel others should obey. And so the breeding ground for all sorts of wheeling and dealing has been created. It is hardly surprising that people who lack a strong foundation fall victim to the many temptations of the current over-ripe capitalism. They all decide to "take care of themselves now," but forget their social and long-term responsibilities. And so super heroes have turned into super grabbers and many people are living at odds with themselves and with society.

The origins of recovery are locked in the biological core of human beings. People can lose contact with it, but sooner or later it returns. By nature, a human-being is not egotistical nor is he inclined to neglect his own sort. He wants to prove his own value and make a contribution to the whole. In the process of self-realization, he may push the limits and test the boundaries, but not at the cost of everything. He is co-operative by nature and will ultimately strive for unity and regularity. That is in his genes. A complementary factor is his intellect which encourages him to create order from chaos. But that is only possible with shared and binding values and norms.

That is why it is so important to keep talking about these things, both with other people and in organizations. In addition, it is important that people develop their inner strength so that they can be armed against their own vulnerability. For as the industrial era is now behind us and the era of external control is fading away, the main question that arises is whether the dependence on such an external control can be replaced by an inner control, an inner voice, the conscience. Because you can obey in two different ways: by following your own moral standards or following those laid down by somebody else. And anybody who cannot command themselves will naturally adhere to the ruling power.

The assignment here is to create a sufficient balance between individual independence and involvement in and care for the surroundings. It is similar to the tension that is maintained in a love relationship between autonomy and intimacy. Only then does self-management offer any perspective.

THE RELEVANCE OF SELF-MANAGEMENT

"If you don't manage, you will be managed."

The transition from the industrial to the information and communication era drastically changed the (power) relationship between politicians and citizens, employers and employees, and suppliers and customers. One of the consequences of this is a shift from a life that was managed and organized for us to one in which everybody is responsible for shaping his or her own future.

A number of factors contribute to this assertion of independence:

- Times have changed. The time when citizens and employees had to be shown the right way to the good life by those above them has long passed. Direction or management from a central position is no longer possible. Policy is now formed in a varied public domain in which discussion, consultation, debate, negotiation, and decision-making all have a place. A rag-tag collection of largely temporary coalitions between the various government and management layers makes sure that the work actually gets done. A governmental and management reality has been created in which people think in terms of processes, arrangements, and functions rather than in structures, layers, and responsibilities.
- Internet has pervaded society. It is anarchical, self-regulating, fragmented, and ignores borders. It has no central cockpit from which everything is managed. The customer – who used to be thought of as king – now emerges as a ruthless killer. He has immediate access to price/quality comparisons and he readily joins other consumers to form a tight front in the price war.
- Talent has gained power. Despite the present economic problems, there is still a big demand for highly-educated personnel. As the population continues to get (on average) older, then the current scarcity in the employment market will become the rule rather than the exception.
- Information is more readily available, real-time and on-line, to everybody who has access to it.
- The labor market is more highly educated than ever before. Today's knowledgeable worker is quite capable of deciding how to improve quality and productivity. Constant innovation and learning are essential. They can even decide on this and manage it themselves.
- It is more about people than about policy. There are no more major issues or, if they occur, they can no longer be solved through centralized political management. What's more, the ideas for such solutions emerge from all the parties in the political spectrum.

■ Little is predictable these days; things are largely unexpected. Just think of the effects terrorism has had on the world and its economy.

If we review all these developments, then our only conclusion can be that these are extremely difficult times for control freaks, centralists, perfectionist, rationalists, planners, and anybody wanting to avoid uncertainty.

These are, therefore, difficult times for managers and politicians who have grown accustomed to approaching reality with a patriarchal and hierarchical mentality and with the accompanying long-term strategies. For others, the confrontation with the characteristics of our current era can also be difficult to deal with and causes a nervous (and nerve-racking) re-evaluation process. We no longer have an effective external authority to which we can entrust our salvation. Even if this power still actually exists, it would be better if we did not become dependent on it.

EMOTIONAL SELF-MANAGEMENT

"I can think and feel whatever I want." – René Diekstra

And so we arrive at the importance of self-management; the ability to decide for yourself what you do and how you react emotionally to an event, regardless of the intensity of the trigger that causes the release of adrenaline. This quality arises from the ability to place emotional reactions in a framework of personal principles, aims, and the associated inner guiding lights. The key to maturity is emotional self-management. This all boils down to taking responsibility for your emotions. In this way of thinking, emotions can never be an excuse for unfruitful behavior. Losing your control is the result of a choice, namely whether you are prepared to give yourself over to an all-powerful primitive feeling. This idea is, of course, completely at odds with the more current way of thinking that says it is "logical" to lose control under certain circumstances. "I was attacked, so I had to defend myself."

Living with honesty as the best policy does not mean answering every question posed to you totally honestly nor does it give you the right to use honesty as a tool to hurt others. Embracing and incorporating honesty as the best policy means being truthful with yourself and with you own values. Take for example a situation that arose in World War Two. When the Nazis came to the door of many people's homes looking for Jews and asked directly if there were any Jews there. The person who is indeed helping a Jewish family hide from the enemy can feel perfectly righteous and honest to themselves and their values when answering "No!"

Keep in mind the big picture, your inner emotions, in order to maintain truthful self-management.

FEELING AT HOME IN YOUR INNER THEATER

"Treat somebody as the person he is and he'll stay that way; treat somebody as the person he could be, and he will become who he is supposed to be."
– Goethe

Our self-image largely determines our way of acting and how we experience things. It is a program of which we are not always conscious; it is built up from previous experiences and from attitudes that we have developed from the feedback we have received. Based on this, an inner voice (interior monologue) develops and a relationship with the outside world is formed. The self-image does not, therefore, only influence our own attitude, but also our behavior towards other people.

A weak self-image ("I hope that they do not notice my mediocrity") or an over-developed one ("I am Napoleon") both negatively affect the relationship with others. A healthy self-image includes the following ingredients:

- *Unconditional self-acceptance*: "I allow myself to be; I do not need to prove anything. I have the inborn right to exert influence and share my unique qualities and inspiration with others. I need not be afraid to take my piece of the pie."
- *Unconditionally positive about myself*: "I am a constructive and loving person on my way to my own destiny. I want to contribute to the emergence of a better world. When I run up against my own boundaries or make mistakes, then I have compassion with myself and try to learn from the experience."
- *Unconditionally positive about others*: "When I think badly of others, I pollute my own mind. I am not judgmental. My initial attitude is one of open expectancy. The other is also doing his or her best to be a good person."

It is extremely important to be able to live with your own reflection. If you cannot love yourself, it is impossible to enter into equal relationships. The challenge is to remain open for feedback and at the same time to remain captain of your own ship. This is difficult, because not everybody is capable of giving sufficient and constructive feedback. It is therefore vital to place reactions in a suitable perspective. This demands self-management and a sense of reality. And don't forget: if you do not manage yourself, somebody else will manage you instead. Too many people seem to be made up of and to live according to the prejudices of others.

True self-respect comes from inside and is all about self-determination, inner peace, independence, and justifiable pride about your contribution to the whole. If this is under control, then it is relatively easy to deal with adversity or obstruction. Because no matter what happens, it is just a problem ... a temporary problem, that can at the most influence a stage in our lives but never our course.

MAKING CLEAR WHAT YOU STAND FOR

"If you light a tiny candle in a dark and dismal room, the light will penetrate into every single corner." – Bernard Lievegoed

In times past, the collective defined rules and regulations for the individual, and the latter thought it more or less natural to obey them. Now the individual wants, to a large degree, to determine his or her own course and give form to his or her life. In practice, we see that rules that are thought to be insignificant or senseless are ignored on a large scale or even sabotaged. In this new world that puts such a premium on self-development, it is becoming increasingly important to know what you stand for, what qualities you, as a person, contribute to the whole, and what you consider important norms and values. This awareness helps you – particularly in turbulent times – to set and maintain course for your own life, to take the right decisions, and to enter into meaningful relationships with the world around you. It is difficult to direct and manage yourself without this awareness. You then become more or less a rubber ball that floats on the waves caused by others. What's more, self-realization must go hand in hand with self-responsibility. Otherwise the self-realization could get out of control and take on the form of egocentricity, self-deception, and opportunism.

It is therefore vital to clearly identify what you stand for and what life you would like to create for yourself and with others. The following questions can be of assistance in a necessary period of reflection:

Private matters

- Why am I here on earth?
- What are my specific qualities and talents?
- What is my "dark side," where is my Achilles heel?
- How would I like to be remembered if, tomorrow, I was no longer here?
- What would I do if I only had one more year to live?

- What gives energy and what drains energy?
- What, as manager of Me Inc., would I most like to change?
- What price am I prepared to pay for this?
- Where in my life is there still a theme that needs further elaboration?

Business matters

- What relationship do my talents and ideals have to my business activities?
- What would I, as president, renew first in my organization?
- What price am I prepared to pay for the realization of my ideals?
- What would I do if I were required to restrict myself to one single professional activity?

It is sensible if you do not try to answer these existential questions now in a clear and immutable way. These are questions that will continue to concern you and the answers will keep developing as long as personal growth continues. But pondering such questions creates inner beacons that can help keep the ship on course. They are conscious moments that separate the essential from the non-essential.

Whatever lights up inside us in such moments has the character of a beacon. If in this way people can get closer to their true selves, then they are better able – if not automatically – to feel what is right and what is wrong. An inner voice develops, a conscience and councilor. The measure of truth does not lie outside yourself, but rather in the feeling that you are one with yourself.

People who feel at ease with themselves will not easily feel the temptation to take liberties with the truth. They do not play a role, but are instead constantly real and present for the full 100 percent. They are unique and special, and at the same time normal and not special. "A little white lie" for such people, is a lie against inner truthfulness and credibility. It clearly shows that the heart finds it more difficult to tell a lie than the intellect.

"You must be the change you wish to see in the world." – Mahatma Gandhi

It is as clear as day that we live in a culture with a strong emphasis on conformity. How often does a child hear: "A rule is a rule" and how often do adults find themselves in the position where they do what is expected of them rather than what they really want. The question arises whether it is at all possible, as an individual, to follow your heart and keep to your own track. We think it is (otherwise we wouldn't have written this book) and we have a number of reasons for this:

- People have souls, they have dreams, ideals, and desires, and can explore them.
- People have a natural desire to be in touch with themselves, and to develop relationships with others, on a deep level as well as for comradeship.
- People have an inborn ability to make choices based on free will and thus help to create the desired reality.
- People are predestined to challenge limits and push back boundaries.
- People tend to resist rules and boundaries that they don't understand.

In short, we are born to be social architects, to create structures from the bottom up not top down.

In giving shape to our personal contribution to society, we can distinguish three levels of ambition:

LEVEL OF AMBITION	AIM	SOURCE	MOVEMENT
Continue	Maintain	Habit	Stay at home
Improve	Expand	Increasing insight	Travel
Renew	Transform	Own needs/ideals	Nomad

The social architect improves and renews, not only because of his ambition, but also out of respect for the inborn creative abilities. In his book *The Answer to How is Yes*, Peter Block clarifies in an impressive way that personal transformation arises more from analyzing the proper questions than from looking for practical solutions. In his vision, it is important that we train ourselves to ask the right questions at the right time. In order to gain insight into our own life story, then *why questions* are far more important than the more popular *how questions* in our surroundings. And there are three reasons for this:

- A "how question" places the attention outward and what's more provokes the person answering to adopt an expert-like attitude.
- An answer that deals with a "how question" is based on the experiences of the person answering and not the person asking the question.
- Many people actually want to arrive at the answers themselves so it may not be prudent to have asked someone else the question in the first place.

In a certain sense, everybody wrestles with his or her own "whys." And that is life's intention. For as soon as we start interfering with each other's "whys," this quickly results in a mental colonialism and the inborn ability for self-management and self-direction is neither consulted nor activated.

Since archaic mindsets can cause situations to spiral into extreme forms, the need for a radical and transparent position increases. The term radical is used here to mean that our own behavior, no matter what the pressures from opposition is, remains connected to our own sense of emotional reality. We need to have the courage to *radically* change the mindset. The better this reality is understood and trusted, the greater our ability to exert effective influence on our fellow man.

Finally, here are a number of tips for those moments when you are under extreme pressure and need to remind yourself that honesty is the best policy:

- Stay in touch with your own deepest knowledge, desires, and ideals
- Trust your own eyes and intuition
- Look for and exercise your freedom; don't complain or sit and wait for permission
- Be accountable
- Search for depth and look at details in interaction
- Become an activist; in any case be clear and transparent about what you want
- Make no distinction any more between what you want and what you think/feel.

In the reality of management and society, it will not always be easy to assert yourself and express your own true emotions. But if we remain silent, we will become increasingly trapped. Accept that you face things alone. And, during the process, do not expect any prize for perfection. The most important thing is that, at the end of the day, you are able to look yourself straight in the eye. Because no punishment meted out by another can possibly be worse than one you give to yourself by contributing to your own degradation! And what is there really to stop you from living with full conviction and total trust in your own ideals and ambitions?

PERSONAL RESPONSIBILITY MODEL

> *"Guilt is a loaded term. But even more loaded – if that is possible – is the term responsibility. In general, people seem to prefer to be guilty of something than to accept the responsibility for it. Responsibility suggests an active attitude, a burden that will have to be carried constantly. Guilt is forgiving and easily atoned. You have to accept responsibility; guilt is just something you get."* – Aliza Tekofsky

The French writer Flaubert believes that tasks are divided between the Lord and mankind: the one is responsible for the beginning and the end, the other for the intervening period. Thus, we are confronted with the absolute responsibility for everything between the beginning and the end. What's more, it is a completely personal responsibility, one that cannot be fobbed off on another. The results of the choices made are one's own, even if they are merely adequate and the consequences of them uncomfortable. And so we come up against one of the major paradoxes of responsibility. Almost everybody is concerned with personal responsibility or actively trying to expand that responsibility, but few are prepared to accept the consequences arising from this. This is all because responsibility means: being visible, being able to make wrong choices, being vulnerable in public, being the fall-guy, and being rejected or excluded. That is why people are rather ambiguous about accepting and certainly taking responsibility.

And yet nobody can avoid taking responsibility for designing their own lives and we all have to deal with the results of our choices and the consequences associated with them. Or to put it more proactively: the quality of life is determined by the quality of the choices we make. Given this importance, it is crucial that we raise the awareness of our own inner steering mechanisms and patterns and those moments of choice that are part and parcel of life.

*Steps in the personal responsibility model**

- First, it is important to be aware of the situation and the current choices.
- A moment of choice is a moment of integrity, in which a whole range of personal values, norms, and ethical convictions meet each other and in which the main question is whether you can remain true to yourself.

* Derived from the personal accountability model of IMPAQ.

PERSONAL RESPONSIBILITY MODEL

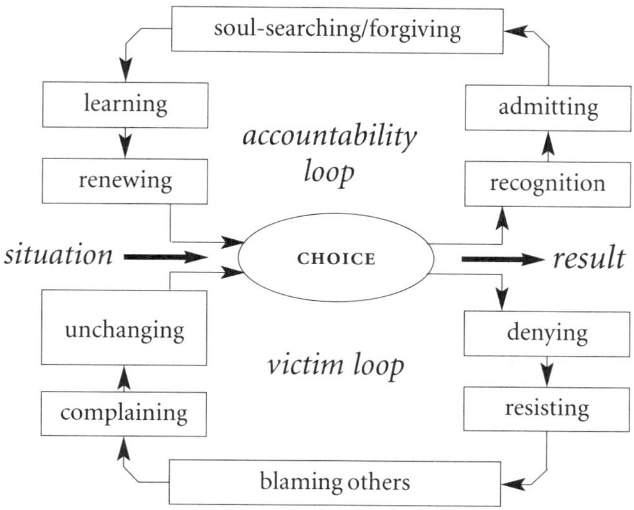

- When there is a choice whether to "face the problems or deny them," it is vital to have the courage to recognize and experience that there is a relationship between your behavior and the current problem (*recognition of the problem*). An additional advantage is that you will ultimately become adept at recognizing this relationship before you make the choice and be able to circumvent many problems at the start. That way, an uncomfortable situation can be avoided and does not digress into a natural disaster making the only solution to clear up the mess.
- However, as the awareness that the problem has a relationship with one's own behavior increases, so does the emotional discomfort. Who really wants to be reminded of his or her own imperfections or be considered the cause of problems? And yet it is important to believe that honesty is the best policy and not flee into denial or opposition.

- Now we are approaching the turning-point in the process and it is time to undertake an in-depth investigation into which personal characteristics, patterns, and problem-maintenance mechanisms have caused the emergence and possible growth of the problems (*self-analysis*). In order to avoid getting bogged down in complaining and self-pity, it is important to develop a productive attitude towards your own imperfection (*forgiveness*).
- Now that you have insight into the problem and have also been able to place some distance between yourself and the problem, it is possible to approach it on a higher level of consciousness and to think creatively about various alternative solutions (*learning*).
- Armed with these new insights and motivated by inner drive, it will slowly become possible to act more autonomously and thus expand your own limits. You have become a player who is able to place his own stamp on the situation, rather than sitting on the bench waiting for others to take action (*renewal*).

Our life choices are driven on the one hand by our desire for happiness and self-realization, and on the other by our aversion to pain and sorrow. Sometimes a critical analysis of the presumed discomfort can help keep the inner rudder steady. "A person suffers most from the suffering that he fears." Making a choice also implies uncertainty. Because if the result of a choice was obvious from the start, then there would no longer be any choice involved. Then the problem would have solved itself.

Many people try to postpone the moment of choice by using the argument that "they don't yet know what they want." This is, however, seldom the issue. The underlying problem in this situation is often that they do not wish to face the consequences of their choice or pay the price for it. In such a case it is essential to make clear that it is impossible to choose without consequences and that there are better excuses for cultivated indecision and masked fear.

CONSCIOUSLY CHOOSING HONEST AND INTENSE RELATIONSHIPS

"Contact demands an appreciation of differences." – Fritz Perls

Man is, above all, a "social animal." He is not there just for himself but is capable, if he is healthy in mind and body, of making a positive contribution to his surroundings. "Happiness" has, after all, two dimensions: the feeling that you are on your own path (being happy) and the knowledge that this happiness can be shared with others. This attention to the surroundings also applies to the ability to make personal sacrifices for it. These are made – albeit sometimes with reluctance – in order to achieve some so-called supra-personal goal. The ability to enter into and deepen relationships creates a connection within our society. It goes without saying that our home and work situations also profit from our ability for self-relativity and self-sacrifice. Relationships of trust are the cement of our society. But at the same time, there is no area that is more exposed to dishonesty than that of relationships. This behavior can be attributed to a lack of inner discipline or losing one's way. In other words: it is most likely that you have never firmly decided for yourself what is really important in your life or you are not prepared to make sacrifices for it. In both cases, the result is a kind of chaotic lifestyle.

There are five levels of intensity and integrity through which a relationship, whether it be personal or work related, can move:*

Exploitation Hidden agendas dominate the nature of this kind of relationship. People use each other and the relationship is purely functional. Everybody is on their guard and feels unsafe, but nobody dares to raise the real issues.

Tolerance Here we tolerate each other and are ruled by the silent agreement: you won't make things difficult for me, and I won't

* Model developed in collaboration with Wessel Ganzevoort.

RELATIONSHIP LADDER

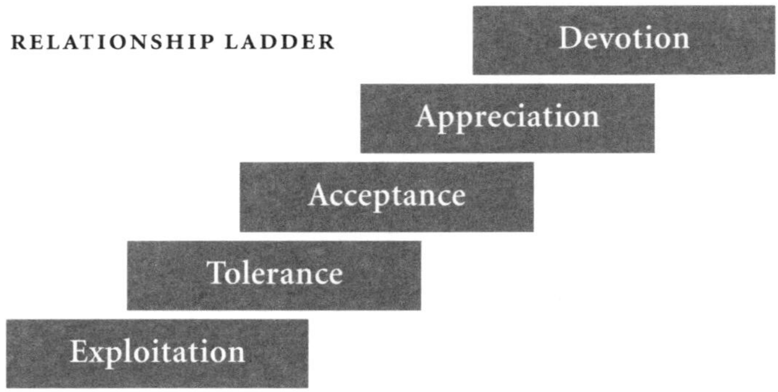

make them difficult for you, and together we'll cover everything. Informal relationships can still be quite pleasant, but once we start dealing with things that really matter, then contacts become largely formal and distant.

Acceptance Participants look each other in the eye, get on well with each other, and know how to evaluate each other. Everybody takes good care of themselves and there is not too much involvement in each other's area of responsibility.

Appreciation People feel real involvement with each other's professional and personal well-being. There is a growing readiness to rise above each other's areas of responsibility and to share scarce resources with each other.

Devotion Within a relationship this implies a deep emotional connection and sharing. People are open-hearted, and know and take into consideration each other's strengths and weaknesses. In other words: they share together their ups and downs.

In all this, the main question is once again what sorts of relationships you want to develop. Do you have a basic trust in the other? What risks would you dare to take and what investment are you prepared to make? But also: do you dare to say goodbye? Because one thing that is all too apparent in the relationship area is that relationships, on the whole, are entered into relatively lightly but can only be ended with the greatest difficulty and when there is no other choice.

Without a sufficient basis of trust and an open and transparent individual contribution, any relationship will, by definition, lose its balance. And this inevitably leads to feelings of disquiet. Then it becomes clear that the core of real individual independence is not that everybody can do as they please. The true essence is being capable of reaching a decision based on a free and inner choice, keeping in mind what contribution the choice will make towards the greater whole.

EXCEL OR COMPETE

"It is never too late to be what you might have been." – George Elliot

We live in a condition of constant superficiality. We flutter like butterflies over the surface, from incident to incident, from sensation to sensation. This means that people seldom take the opportunity to do some inner reflection, pose important questions, and search for depth. Mostly we do not see ourselves for who we really are and what we want to achieve. Rather, we have accepted as a matter of course that the best way to prove ourselves is by achieving aims that have been set by others. At times we even find ourselves living according to rules that we consider senseless. This observation suggests the thought that self-determination has never been so necessary, yet at the same time has never been so discouraged.

An important step towards real independence and sovereign self-determination is made when people choose to listen to their own conscience and to live according to inner convictions. It is all about making a choice between *excelling* and *competing*.

On an *individual level, excelling* means: determining your own aims, going for your own gold, following your conscience, being unequal, making a difference, leaving both past and compromise behind. It also means being deeply connected with your surroundings and looking for this contact from your own inner strength, without making concessions to your own level of ambition or your own conscience. Your self-image is not or no longer derived from recent performance or material possessions, but rather from constantly feeling good about yourself. You are no longer dependent on the evaluation your surroundings make of you and, no matter what happens, always return to the real you.

On an *organizational level, excelling* means: creating markets, continuous improvement and revitalization, being the benchmark, creating added value, and making use of all the available talent and potential. In short: doing more than the customer expects and no longer following others in the market. Excellent companies offer room for individual excellence, but at the same time keep their eyes on the whole. Synergy and process-directed activities are specifically encouraged. It is all for one and one for all. Confrontations and conflicts are part and parcel of this striving for excellence and are actively acknowledged. Compromises are avoided as much as possible, because these can only lead to a commitment that is mediocre and half-hearted.

People who *compete* with each other and with their surroundings ultimately create win–lose relationships in their surroundings. They do not play their own game, but allow themselves to be dictated to by their surroundings. If you have performed well then you are worthwhile. But the performance is based on other people's expectations. And interestingly, because the rules are set by others even when you do compete and win, the victory can taste bitter and your feeling of self-worth can get dented. In organizations, too, *competing* can be highly prized but since it generally involves competing with everyone for the scarce resources: promotions, prestige, and money, it takes a significant toll on all personal and professional relationships. This transcends the boundaries within and ultimately can affect the relationship the company has with its customers. That is why being focused on competition can actually be one of the greatest handicaps for an excellent performance towards customers and the market.

When we talk of excelling, we talk about high achievement, something usually attributed to "the competitive edge." However, we do not simply mean excelling by 10 percent, but rather looking at the situation 100 percent differently. Faced with a challenge, the high-flyers see opportunities and the conservatives see restrictions. The one becomes active, the other passive. That is why the inner choice for excellence is so vital. Excelling means reaching the highest goal you set for yourself. Competition means reaching the highest goal someone else sets.

THE LAWS OF THE HEART

"The heart has its reasons, of which Reason knows nothing." – Blaise Pascal

Important life decisions are largely taken on the basis of intuition. There is nothing wrong with that. It is inadvisable to act in conflict with your feelings. There is a lot of wisdom and life experience in what we call intuition. "It doesn't feel right" is a legitimate strategy. What's more, such a sentence forces the person to go in search of a rational motivation and this can usually be found. The quality of our life is not determined by what we think, but by the way we experience the situation.

Feelings color the individual and, as long as they are accepted and properly evaluated, they can make an impact on the situation. When rationale and emotion are extensions of each other and mind and heart are in harmony, this, coupled with being positive can create an impact that will never be forgotten. Conversely, denying feelings can also color a situation, but then negatively. When a pattern is developed of continually ignoring emotions, people become flat and restrained, like a conjuror with a living disappearing act. It is rational recklessness to think that emotions are unimportant – even if people do their best to hide their feelings (vulnerability) behind a mask of rational indifference. Sooner or later, this causes not only a feeling that you are wearing an iron mask, but also superficial relationships with yourself and the world around you. In this way of life, people are simply passers-by: they come and they go. He may do his best, but he is lost.

The rationalist does what Chinese parents used to do with their daughters. When the fashion of the time dictated small feet, the parents achieved this by tightly binding the feet. The result: women were doomed to hobble for the rest of their lives. The same fate threatens people who think they can ignore the laws of the heart.

Practical tips

- *Test your feelings* at each important decision. Think of a decision in which you ignored your feelings. They are seldom the happiest decisions. If your feeling says: this deal is not okay, then at least take a look at the feeling.
- *Be explicit about your interests and needs*; don't sit around thinking that others will understand what you need. Don't talk in terms of standpoints, but talk instead about the underlying feelings, needs, and interests. Wordless deals contain the source of disappointment.
- *Don't think for somebody else and assume you know their response*; it is arrogant and wastes energy. It leads to unexamined assumptions, misunderstandings, feelings of guilt, and negative anticipation.
- *Make sure your own emotional matters are in order*. If you live your life to the fullest, then it is naturally the intention that you share this with somebody else. In this way of sharing, you will not lose yourself.

If somebody does not learn to talk about desires and feelings during emotionally quiet times, then this ability will break down when it is needed most. Think, for example, of emotional need in times of dealing with death, dismissal, or pension. Many take their pension and then discover that the situation at home has been neglected and that the career had been a ticking time-bomb rather than a source of permanent life involvement.

Another important aspect is keeping the equilibrium of give and take in a relationship. If someone takes too much at the beginning, then their behavior soon becomes egocentric and does not invite cooperation. It is, however, equally unwise to giving without limits and not to express sufficiently one's own interests and feelings. The best perspective is offered by keeping your eye on your own interests and on those of others. The commitment grid of Geoff Bellman attempts to display this:

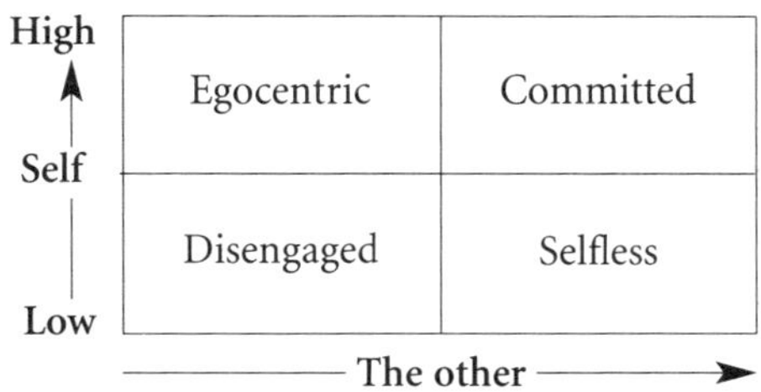

LIVING WITH YOUR OWN HYPOCRISY

"Let him who is without sin throw the first stone."

Although the title, *Honesty: The Best Policy* suggests a preferred perspective, this book is not a plea for a perfect life made up of nothing but completely honest decisions. Realizing such a high ideal is not something that most of us will ever fully achieve. What's more, placing too much emphasis on perfection will inevitably lead to hypocrisy. When problems arise, it will only emphasize the tendency for denial and rationalization.

Thus you do not need to be perfect before you have the right to discuss things in the area of honesty. For who is without sin? There will always be moments in your life when it is extremely difficult to maintain the inner rudder on its proper course. But as long as you don't expect everything you do to be perfect, then there is no need for pretence, and there is room for development. By looking carefully at your own learning assignment, it becomes easier to accept the problems somebody else may have with integrity. It is important to be forgiving of others, so that you don't feed the hypocrisy by making value judgments and projections. Be aware that it is nonsense to think that the ability to cause harm is only present in somebody else.

It is much healthier to address your own fears, and your aggressive and animal tendencies. The more we are able to do this and the better our conscience works, the less chance there is for dishonesty. In his book *Change the World*, Robert Quinn emphasizes the importance of unconditional trust. If we have this, then we can, as it were, learn something from any situation. "People who have such trust, consider themselves capable of ditching incorrect assumptions and ineffective strategies while they are right in the middle of the process."

It is not therefore necessary – and it could also be boring – to be as straight as an arrow all the time. If we occasionally go off the rails, then our sense of shame will quickly get us back on track. Shame works in the soul as a spontaneous feeling that arises when you treat yourself or somebody else unjustly. This signal reminds you that you are not living according to your moral standards and it mobilizes your consciousness to do things better the next time.

COURAGE

"There is only one quality worse than hardness of heart and that is softness of head." – Teddy Roosevelt

Achieving revitalization means leaving the old road and letting go of old securities. This can cause a feeling of homelessness which in turn can make us yearn for the old trusted situation. Once we have arrived at this point, we are faced with a *moment of choice* about change: *Should I do it or not?* These sorts of moments that occur daily determine the quality of life. It demands courage, bravery and daring to look this in the eye – plus a whole lot of other similar qualities – if we are to make the right choice. A painful side-effect is that if no choice is made, then the situation will make the choice for you. And you lose the chance of self-direction. Thus it is good to take a look at the virtue that makes such action possible: courage. Courage has two underlying qualities:

- *The absolute will (commitment)* to live according to your own convictions, values and norms. In this approach to life, there is not the slightest gap between behavior and the underlying principles. The will is fed by an inner motor, and the person requires no outside stimuli to motivate action.
- *The daring and discipline* to do what is necessary and to resist escape mechanisms such as the tendency to succumb to pressure, to deny, or to rationalize.

A courageous person is able to live a principled life, because he is able to overcome fears and suppress the urge to flee. He knows that uncontrolled anger is the greatest obstacle to self-direction and for a happy and social life. He is, just as everybody else, sometimes scared or fearful, but he is able to stop this from playing a decisive role.

People with insufficient inner strength cannot offer resistance to less effective urges within themselves (for example, indolence or helplessness) or negative urges in others (for example, dominance).

They became the toy of their fearful or often self-imagined suspicions and anticipate all possible forms of calamity. They cannot be generous, because they are afraid of not having enough for themselves. They cannot be just, because they are too scared to stand up to anything themselves. And even if they want to act in accordance with their own rules, this too is a problem because they do not really know what they stand for or are unable to master their own fears.

The following tips are for people who could use a little more courage in their lives:

- *Stop the self-recrimination and self-punishment*; people do not become more courageous by assuming they are cowards. Try to be compassionate here and control impatience.
- *Resist the inclination to exaggerate risks*; this causes an increased tension that makes it unpleasant to take any sort of action. Divide a large step into a series of smaller steps and enjoy every success on the way to the final goal. People become more daring from success than from failure.
- *Learn to talk about feelings and underlying fears* when things are going well; people become a lot less lonely when they discover that other people share the same anxieties. It is advisable to learn this before there is a crisis.
- *Practice makes perfect*; learn to be more daring by testing your limits in relatively safe circumstances. Here, again, success does a lot for self-confidence.
- *Make an effort and dig deeper than normal*; discipline is an important factor in any form of behavior or pattern change. Indolence is the principle opponent. Instead of letting opposition or setbacks stop you, see the difficulty as a challenge.

Although some people project through their behavior a different image of themselves, there is nobody who does not know fear. Those who suggest otherwise often allow themselves to be ruled by the fear of being seen as scared. The question is not whether life can be led without fear. The decisive question is how we handle pain, fear, and sorrow. Because although pain and sorrow are inevitable in our lives, suffering is a choice.

Having the courage to change your approach, to break free from the same old patterns, is an essential step in your journey towards a new awareness. The time has come to take responsibility for yourself, your actions and your values. Become immune to dishonesty by finding your inner truth.

4

FALLEN HEROES

"An important question is whether life at the top leads to a top life."

CURRENT TIMES make totally new demands on people and leaders within an organization. Industrial thinking from the past century has made way for a fundamentally different view on companies: organizations as living and learning organisms.

At the beginning of the previous century, Barnard suggested that a subordinate's decision on whether to obey or disobey an order determines the authority of that order. In other words: it is the subordinate who decides whether the leadership has any authority or not. In industrial organizations, the consequences of following an order or not usually become evident quite quickly. But in our current era, it is becoming increasingly unclear where and how value is created in organizations. Orders can be delayed temporarily or permanently, or even substantially changed. If those in charge are unaware of this or do not know how to deal with it, then they will certainly be faced with it soon enough.

There is now an organizational context in which self-determination, entrepreneurial behavior, and the readiness to change, set the scene. Hierarchical-flavored organizational forms are being replaced by alliances, partnerships, and network relationships. In this new world, the quality of personal contribution, certainly for those in charge, is becoming crucial. Because without adding the necessary vision and drive, self-determination does not lead to productivity, entrepreneurial behavior does not lead to results, and a readiness to change does not lead to movement. Leaders are now expected to lead the way in achieving and accelerating the change processes. Sometimes they even have to go against the tide and against the conformists. They must be sovereign, courageous, and consistent.

But they do not need to be Superman, constantly "setting a good example" and "pulling the organization through." These are examples of "I attack – follow my example" concepts from times past, with as underlying idea the conviction that the sheep will always follow the shepherd. This is no longer the case. What's more, many shepherds collapse under the high expectations that the various stakeholders around them have. It is thus high time for the development and adoption of a more horizontal perspective about leading and being led.

Subordinates also need to set aside the prevalent patriarchal thinking about leading and being led. That takes effort, because everybody is accustomed to operating in a dependency relationship. What's more, people are spoiled, because it is relatively easy in such a relationship to point to somebody else and to avoid any personal responsibility for a choice. If things get difficult, you can always say that the real problem is caused by management and that you are simply following orders. The relationship between boss and subordinate in the industrial era was not very demanding on the worker. Now that we live in a different age, it is vital to emphasize the responsibility for and the consequences of one's own choices. And we must gradually develop a new language for the relationship and interaction between "boss" and "worker." There are virtually no terms that adequately describe these new relationships. "Superior" and "subordinate" are no longer appropriate, certainly not in a professional environment. Similarly, "the boss and his people" implies more authority and ownership rights than are justified by reality. We could try to use the word "colleague," but then it is essential that we develop the appropriate behavior towards each other.

FROM SUPER-HERO TO SUPER-GRABBER

"Managers are increasingly acting as if they own the company, when in fact they are simply on the pay-roll."

No role is more susceptible to inflation in social status and value than that of a (top) manager. Those admired and even deified leaders of the (post) industrial period have, in no time, become trivial and sometimes even despised figures. The press even talks of "grabbers" and "unguided missiles." Of course, such descriptions do not do justice to the greater majority of leaders. But just as we must learn to be more realistic about the share prices of a company, so must we be more realistic about our leaders. As status disappears, so too does the unrealistic expectations about the functioning of leaders. For it must be lonely and almost unbearable to have to live up to the expressed and unexpressed expectations of those around you. It must be remembered that it is not so much the leader as a person, but rather the strength of the collective that leads to action and revitalization.

Leaders are not miracle workers, nor do they need to be. They are "normal people" with extra responsibility. They have the same desires, fears, and obstacles as "normal people." Thanks to their role, they are simply legitimized in advance about concerning themselves with the functioning of the organization. In the new thinking about leading and being led, however, everybody has this privilege and thus the rigid division between steering and being steered is swept away.

THE LEADER AS A GOOD HOST

"I want to live in a universe that I trust so much that I can stop playing God Almighty." – Margareth Wheatley

So many bosses, so many deviations. What do you think of all those top managers who announce massive redundancies and at the same time give themselves large raises and arrange for themselves lucrative option packages? Or what do you think of those top managers who put their profits up, exaggerate their turnovers, and conjure away their losses? You need guts for that, particularly now when it is becoming increasingly obvious that a company's results are just as dependent on external factors (economy, interest rate, consumer confidence, the Dow Jones and FTSE) as they are on the quality of management decisions. You have to wonder whether these people have a screw loose! Another explanation is that the constant pressure to achieve higher turnover and higher profits has been so alienating that these people have lost touch with their own conscience. This is certainly the case with people with a very tiny sense of personal value or a very large inferiority complex. For if somebody is empty inside, then there is a very good chance that this must be compensated from the outside through megalomanic behavior and an associated recklessness.

Since today "more of the same" is no longer acceptable, we have to search for a "different sort of more." Margareth Wheatley explains the necessary turnabout like this: "A leader no longer needs to play the hero, but rather the good host." And, as behooves a good host, make sure that people in his surroundings feel at ease, are comfortable, and enjoy visiting. The most effective leaders at the moment are those that know perfectly well what they want, but also look for connections to the ambitions and desires of colleagues and others involved.

They are capable of revealing hidden possibilities and thus facilitate people in achieving the best possible level of performance. They do what is good for the company and keep their eye on the longer term. They do this patiently, carefully, and step by step; their behavior is subdued and sympathetic, rather than loud and compelling. They pay attention to company politics without getting lost in them or resorting to unethical behavior. In other words, they know that they only have their power "on loan." Modern management virtues are independence, self-control, modesty, helpfulness, and tenacity.

Effective leaders are comfortable with themselves as people and have an above-average awareness of their own drives, qualities, and inadequacies. Because of this, they are more balanced and predictable in a pleasant way. In confrontations or in setbacks, their behavior remains consistent. In short: it is good to work with and for such a person.

An important reason why "heroes" have such a difficult time at the moment is that organizations today are complex technological and management constructions. Somebody who wants to bring about change by acting like John Wayne ("my way or the high way") is doomed to failure. If somebody really wants to help bring about a meaningful change, then he must first fully understand the existing complexity and involve people as much as possible in the creation of and responsibility for the change process.

For those who are not prepared to make such a deep investment, it is inadvisable to have the ambition to become manager or consultant in a large company. Of course it can be psychologically attractive for somebody to suggest to the world that he is able to perform miracles. But fundamentally improving the health of an organization demands, in practice, more exertion than their patience or nervous system can take. Perhaps change is also possible for them, for example by accepting a compromise in a crisis of confidence. Or because they become aware that their private life is suffering too much because of the role they are playing.

FATHERS FROM THE PAST

> *"Most leaders act like fathers from the past. While the flood is rising around them, they are still occupied with fortifying the sandcastles. In the meantime, their children are carrying on with the game elsewhere."*

A major misunderstanding that is affecting the behavior of people today is the assumption that an organization can only achieve some form through decisions made at the top. This idea is, in today's communication and information era, no longer true or desirable. This way of looking at things only hinders the emergence of a more current and real image of the world today. Within our out-of-control environment full of unexpected developments, an organization actually steers itself. And, just as in the real world, life in organizations takes on a whole range of guises. A hierarchical description of this is the simplest, but possibly the least true. Most organizations operate despite, rather than because of, management and its retinue. And yet, management still claim ownership of internal roles and changes made to them, and insist on representing the organization to the outside world. Because of their pride, management place themselves above and outside organizational reality. By doing this, it doesn't only obstruct itself, but also inhibits the forces of emancipation and change. As long as the industrial age way of thinking about management still dominates the actual events within an organization, then most motivational and customer-related problems will remained unsolved. That is why most change programs get bogged down in *suspicion*, *powerlessness*, and *cynicism*. Because it is not possible to solve these problems with the same sort of thinking that caused them. Therefore every effective change process must be preceded by a fundamental change of attitude in the main players.

THE PARALYZING FEAR OF CHAOS

"Daring means losing security for a moment;
not daring means losing yourself for ever."

Many revitalization processes are influenced or frustrated by the need (of senior management) to keep the situation under control. Although people say that they really do want to change, the actual process shows a need for clarity, predictability, and controllability. There is even a degree of panic if unexpected events occur or the efforts towards change do not bring about the expected results. For the impression must be avoided at all costs that the center of power has lost control. Once again we see that the need for public relations about a person or project is considered far more important than paying attention to what is actually happening in the organization. And, for the sake of convenience, we ignore the fact that within the organization, despite or indeed because of these efforts to keep control, management and project control are in chaos. The existence of this anarchical situation is generally unnoticed or even denied by the leaders. After all, this situation has never been "formally authorized" by the leadership.

Change activities must always stem from and be directed at influencing reality. And so there is a lot of fundamental realigning and redefining work to be done – certainly if the term "chaos" is still equated with "catastrophe." After all, there is another definition. William Bridges formulated this in 1980 as follows: "Chaos is not a mess, but rather an original form of pure energy to which people return to at every real new beginning." Probably each real revitalization goes hand in hand with much unrest and deep confusion for everyone involved – not least of all, senior management.

The (temporary) discomfort is proof that this time things are for real and that people are prepared to risk high stakes. Chaos and uncertainty are part and parcel of a genuine change process; they stimulate the creative and self-saving abilities and insure that borders are really changed. People who are able to deal with chaos generally demonstrate a well-developed awareness of their own value and for their value on the employment market. They have a clear insight into their own situation, a suitable helicopter view with sufficient distance to place incidents into a larger context, and the ability to request help in time. Leaders would do well to have these qualities. A need for control and a need to keep an eye on everything that is happening is almost always the result of a personal lack of confidence in the self-regulating and self-healing ability of an organization and its employees. What's more, a deep self-analysis and the acceptance of the associated fears results in the ability to set out on an adventure.

It is time for leaders to learn that the "dogma of control" must be set aside and in its place they must learn to accept chaos and the accompanying change dynamics. For ultimately "chaotic activity is always preferable to controlled inactivity" (Weick).

ALL LEADERSHIP IS SHARED LEADERSHIP

"A large group of managers form a significant battalion in the army of the hidden unemployed."

A lot of literature is devoted to remarkable management personalities and their exceptional performance. Jack Welch, Richard Branson, Bill Gates. They are sparkling personalities with a dream, an unusual style of leadership, brilliant ideas, and a sharp business instinct.

ERA	LEADERSHIP	FOCUS	CONTROLLING MECHANISM	ATTITUDE
Communication	Motivator	Cohesion + EQ	Vision	Sincerity
Information	Facilitator	Advancement	Knowledge	Inspiration
Industrial	Manager	Control	Rules	Efficiency
Agricultural	Land Lord	Honor	Authority	Status

In management practice, you do not meet many such people. In fact, most leaders do not characterize themselves as having brilliant ideas, individual prominence, charisma, and daring. With only a rare exception, most leaders are quiet, intelligent, and sensitive to their surroundings; people who, more than anything else, take good care of business as usual and are competent in assessing the feasibility of their plans and finding a suitable consensus for them. If we look at things in this way, then there is a considerable gap between the romanticized image of business heroes and the day-to-day reality of management practice. If we are to bridge this gap, then it is useful to place the ideals into the context of time and company. And once more to look closely at the underlying opinions about leading and being led:

- In the industrial era, the prevalent opinion about leadership was that somebody had to be born to the role. Leadership was seen as a logical result of personal qualities, competencies, and skills. People would talk about "natural leaders." As a consequence, people would question the idea of training leaders: it cannot be learned, just developed.
- In our current era, leadership can also be considered something of interpersonal influence and as the result of a rational negotiation process. In this way of thinking, the need for leadership arises during a cooperative process and, in a certain sense, leaders are created by a group. Leadership is a role for the most influential person within the given context (company culture). This influence need not go hand in hand with personal charisma. As a consequence of this way of thinking, leadership skills can be learned and developed within the limits of personal potential.

The way we value leadership behavior is thus strongly influenced by time, culture, and context. This explains why organizations and professional sectors have such a diverse range of leadership styles and why there is such a variation in their appreciation. Behavior that is highly valued in one organization may be ridiculed or even unaccepted in another company. A good illustration of the way culture determines the value of leadership is this comment made within a governmental organization: "Some managers here are like nonentities. That's fine, just as long as they themselves are aware of it and don't blame others."

MAKING ROOM FOR THE DIFFERENT MANAGEMENT TYPES

"Many managers prefer to deal with a problem they cannot solve rather than with one they cannot understand."

In the realization of organizational change, people who want to change something in the *status quo* have a heavier burden of proof than those who want to keep things the way they are. "What on earth is all that good for; aren't things going well as they are...?" Yet in these chaotic times, the risks of stagnation are greater than the risks caused by change efforts that may not be perfect. An organization where everything is (apparently) in order, does not move with its surroundings and is most likely in an advanced state of rigidity. So why this great love of stability and predictability? Perhaps an answer to this can be found by examining the professional training and experience that most leaders have.

Most managers are "originally" economists or engineers and thus carry around with them the associated socialization processes and preoccupations. The economist and engineer share a need to make developments as predictable, as rationally explainable, and as measurable as possible. They love to use instruments, methods, techniques, skills, and to do research into employment satisfaction. They want to show as quickly and objectively as possible that the organization is "on the right track."

The down-side to this way of thinking is that there is often insufficient room for the unpredictable and magical aspects of every change activity. And so many processes prematurely lose their dynamics and vitality because management concentrates on increasing the manageability and/or achieving measurable results.

There is more in heaven and hell than material and measurable progress. And so there must be more room for those qualities that are traditionally associated with the professional backgrounds of psychologists and artists (the archetypes listed below are inspired by the thinking of Peter Block in his book *The Answer to How is Yes*):

- The *engineer* is particularly interested in constructing and designing the world. The key question is almost always how the assignment can be adequately translated in a technical way. Since the object must always be there for a longer time, he chooses the safe way and often overdoes it by building too much structure. This professional group is most interested in predictability and measurable progress. In general, there is not much room for human emotions and frailty. They always want things concrete and tangible.
- The *economist* naturally starts from a scarcity philosophy and asks himself (or herself) what the value of the article or service is, expressed in money or "return on investment." What's more, any transaction ends with the question: What is left on the bottom line, what profits are there after tax, and what leverage has been achieved? In this philosophy, there is little room for those things that cannot be measured such as life happiness and social added value.
- The *psychologist* is particularly focused on understanding the experiential world and increasing the possibility for personal development. For him, it is of primary importance that people are judged on their value and feel happy and are able to develop themselves according to their own abilities. There is a more or less natural resistance against measuring whether psychological efforts have any use. After all, isn't human behavior far too complex to state or even suggest that there is a direct relationship between intervention and its results?
- The *artist* wants to bring about beauty and magic. Standard subjects are rather dull and do not do justice to the uniqueness of any given situation. The artist wants to contribute something beautiful to society and is not really concerned about counting the costs. He is concerned about the aesthetic beauty and the uniqueness of the design. It is all about the experiential reality of those directly involved. For how on earth can you determine the objective beauty of a poem or a piece of art?

■ The *philosopher* is interested in the long term. He sees the big picture. He can follow the line of the strategy and see its potential. Furthermore, the *philosopher* helps to stimulate thought processes and solves problems relating to meaning. He is willing to stretch the limits in the hope that a greater good can be achieved. Boundaries fade away as the philosopher makes his way toward the ultimate goal.

LEADERSHIP ROLES

1	THE ENGINEER *focused on practicality and predictability*
2	THE ECONOMIST *focused on leverage and financial predictions*
3	THE PSYCHOLOGIST *focused on feelings and personal growth*
4	THE ARTIST *focused on beauty and image*
5	THE PHILOSOPHER *focused on the big picture*

Until recently, it was generally economists and engineers who directed the thinking and acting within organizations. This type of thinking has become so dominant that in many ways we have become colonized by it. The endless search for instruments, methods, and techniques has eroded the ability to see and experience what is actually happening in the process on an emotional level. It is high time that more space is given to the psychologist, artist and philosopher types in management. Hopefully then a new type will emerge: a combination of all of them. For it is the broad perspective that fulfills the needs of modern society.

> *"Just imagine that Martin Luther King had shouted: 'I have a dream' and had then just stood around wondering 'I wonder whether this will ever take off.'"*

Many leaders (and many who are led) are caught in a self-strengthening negative spiral. Employees feel they have little room for initiatives or risk-taking and thus show less and less entrepreneurial behavior in their work. For many leaders, this is proof that people cannot accept responsibility and that there should thus be more rules and controls. The fatal by-product of this thinking is that nobody uses his or her brains and every form of entrepreneurial behavior and pro-activity disappears.

It is possible to escape from this spiral, but it requires courage, daring, and persistence. For it is clear that neither leaders nor those they lead can easily escape from established patterns of behavior. In the beginning, it all takes a lot of getting used to and it is, for a sharp observer, quite easy to paralyze the whole process with negative value judgments or personal disqualifications. Perhaps that is why the most important assignment during any change operation is to give each other room for growth and experimentation based on the noble art of forgiveness.

Inspirational and servant leadership is a unique profession. It is personality and talent, rather than expert knowledge, that makes people suitable for leadership activities. In this view of leadership, the following things are important:

- *Authentic behavior.* People do not need to be perfect, but rather realistic, open, and honest. Everybody recognizes the difference between somebody who is passionate and somebody who just "does their work." Similarly, the difference between an inflated know-it-all and somebody solid is also immediately noticeable. Important qualities here are trustfulness, presence of mind, inner peace and cultivation, trust, energy, and passion.
- *Servitude.* Leadership implies the absolute choice for servitude

and helpfulness. The emphasis on perfecting one's own performance has to be transformed into "how can I help the other function better." That is not easy for ego-trippers and career-makers. For many people, it demands a deep re-orientation of one's personal drives and ambitions.

- *Maintaining the "Me Inc."* Servitude does not mean "selling yourself short" nor does it mean paying less attention to yourself. The desire to function in the service of something that is greater than yourself (a supra-personal ideal), demands sufficient self-reflection and attention to the "Me Inc." Giving development help comes easier from inner wealth.
- *Humor and putting things into perspective.* The one thing that you notice in most companies is the terribly serious atmosphere. It's as if everybody has just completed a training course in "looking serious." The correct amount of relaxation, cheerfulness, and the ability to put things into perspective not only make things more enjoyable but also more effective.
- *Communicative and involving ability.* Leadership is largely to do with effective communication. Sharing information is a must and there are countless communication moments in any day. The effective leader is a specialist in communication, both as receiver and transmitter.
- *Availability and approachability.* The super do-it-yourself heroes among leaders make sure that they move from one meeting to another and from one kick to another. This means that there is little time left for communication with those who, according to the social annual report, are the most important source of future success. An effective leader will therefore limit the number of meetings or send representatives to them. In this way, there will be more time for himself and for communicating with the people around him.

In the current situation, leaders are increasingly called upon to make fundamental choices and to take a certain position. They must maneuver between taking risks and leaving everything as it is, between confrontation and manipulation, between servitude and egocentricity. This demands a permanent choice to act with integrity according to your own values and norms. What's more, it is important that you develop a passion for this role. You can expect opposition and you will most probably – at least in the short term – not generate popularity with this. But the role does give you the possibility of influencing those in your direct surroundings to help you create the reality you desire. This requires a personal answer to the following questions:

- What is it that you essentially wish to create in your direct environment/organization and why is this important for you?
- What aims are worth pursuing in your area of responsibility and why is it important to work on them?

Only when you have answered these questions is it interesting to turn your attention to how these aims can be achieved in the most effective and pleasant manner.

GREAT THEORY – BUT IT WOULDN'T WORK HERE

"Success comes in Cans, not in Can'ts."

There are many reasons for not making a choice, or to justify why a particular management theory (including this one) cannot work in your own environment. An important refuge is the nature of the organization and its corporate culture. Of course the strategies, activities, and culture within an energy supplier or city sanitation department will be different to those in an electronics manufacturer, a hotel chain, or a financial service company. Treacey and Wiersema distinguish four strategic alternatives that can allow companies to excel:

- *Operational excellence:* offering quality for the lowest price. This demands focusing on maximum efficiency.

- *Product leadership:* focus on continuous innovation. Customers are prepared to pay a premium because they know that they receive state-of-the-art products and services.
- *Brand championship:* achieving the maximum from the customers' perceived value of the brand. This choice is frequently made by manufacturers of consumer goods.
- *Customer intimacy:* offering a total solution to the customer. They regard the supplier as a problem solver.

There is a typical culture for each of these alternatives. For example, organizations that wish to distinguish themselves in operational excellence and brand championship will generally have a culture of rules. Processes and the way the customer experiences the brand are constantly checked and controlled, particularly centrally. Product leadership requires a culture with values such as creativity, room for experimentation, daring to take risks. Customer intimacy will quickly distinguish itself in a target culture, directed at setting aims, being decisive, and feeling responsible for results.

The question is whether these characteristics form an obstacle to developing a true "self." Naturally, everybody will choose an organization that best fits with his or her own character. At first glance, there will be less room to maneuver in a rules culture than in an innovative culture. And yet we must not allow ourselves to be fooled.

Let us, for the sake of clarity, look at a practical example. It goes without saying that an energy generation plant will need to be manned 24/7. This requires a strict timetable which insures that people are present when needed. But it is quite possible that that timetable can be filled in through mutual discussion and not necessarily be strictly dictated by rules made by those at the top. On the other hand, an innovative culture may appear to offer greater freedom, but there can also be a strong social pressure to move within certain (technical or scientific) paradigms. For several decades, the

American 3M company has tried to circumvent this potential problem by allowing their employees to use a part of their time for their technical hobbies, using company equipment.

It is this sort of practical and concrete solution in the area of freedom and time, that comes from an honest leader and which can have an effect on the spiritual freedom for the employees as well as the managers own "self." It is all about looking for and maximizing personal freedom while still efficiently achieving the goal.

Leaders today need to be flexible, communicative and open. They must think outside the box. A good leader is a motivator with vision but also a human being who cares for and listens to others. Someone who incorporates various approaches including all the management types listed in this chapter. They need to work with the chaos of the ever changing times and not resist it. And those that are led must not stay passive, they need to participate and share in the movement of the organization. Real leadership comes from the support of those that are led. And people nowadays are more critical and knowledgeable than ever before. Strict authority as it was once known has no place anymore in our modern society. That is why the emerging leader is no longer a hero or authoritarian either adored or feared by the masses, but a person who is trusted and respected for his ability and authenticity.

5

CRIMINAL ORGANIZATIONS

"*You get used to anything. That is the trump card held by oppressors and intolerant people. The victim bends but does not break. People adapt in order to survive. And while your view on the world hardens, your pride becomes as soft and malleable as the skull of a new-born baby. While some live in fear and degradation, others can act as if nothing is wrong. It's as simple as that.*" – Arthur Japin

It is hardly surprising that integrity in the sense of consistency and transparency is such an important issue at the moment. And it is also an issue within organizations. For although most organizations are not affected by bookkeeping malpractices or other forms of fraudulent activity, most do suffer from a blurring of norms and self-betrayal. Just look at the amount of haggling that takes place during the annual budget discussions. Or talk to the head of HR about the gap between the reward and assessment policy and the way management implements it. But rather than bothering to ask why the existing instruments are used so inadequately, new ones are developed. Even new control mechanisms are implemented in case these new instruments are not embraced wholeheartedly.

The main problem, however, is seldom caused by a lack of instruments. The real problem goes much deeper and is all about the dated mentality of the people at the top. The belief that people only act because management tells them to. In practice, the opposite generally holds true. People *behave as though* they are motivated and seem, at least at first glance, to be doing what is asked of them. But in the meantime, they just go about their own business. It makes companies seem a bit of a mess. We can put down our observations in two laws. The first is: "Look behind the scenes in an organization – any organization – and you will be sure to find a mess." The second law elaborates on the first: "it is such a mess in organizations because people are not interested in each other, but only in themselves." Endless discussion and consensus seeking, has not done much good in bringing organizations into line. Because although open confrontations are largely avoided, there is a lot of underground tension. What's more, many leaders are discouraged from following their feelings and exerting influence on the situation because of this one-sided emphasis on compromise and consensus.

This culture has resulted in many misplaced "tolerance" policies within companies and has caused a fragmented and diffused responsibility for the cause of the disturbing situation. Thus there is also a need for realignment within organizations. Because if the fundamental problem of an organization is no longer primarily caused by a lack of tools and instruments, then where is the problem? And what can we do to help solve the problem or – and this can have a possible added value –we can try to bring the problem to a higher level of abstraction which may allow it to solve itself!

DESPERATE TIMES AND PRIMITIVE RELATIONSHIPS

"Powerlessness corrupts and leads to violence and bureaucratic behavior."

Just saying what is wrong is simply "not done" in most organizations. You could, after all, harm each other, even though this is not the intention. You prefer to protect each other, because you never know what the future may bring. And it's good to be on your guard where top leaders are concerned, because the chance is very real that your openness will be rewarded with "suitable measures." At the very least, your openness could have consequences for your place in the pecking order. It is a quiet, sometimes silent intimidation. You think that nothing is allowed and act as if you are paralyzed. And so the feeding ground for suffering, quiet opposition, and subtle sabotage is created.

If this anesthetic spreads and takes on a collective character, then everybody starts silently assuming that the system simply can't be repaired. What's more, nobody really expects it to happen. As hope disappears, so too does courage and the readiness to commit yourself to change and make personal sacrifices for it. Nobody feels like the owner of the given situation. Everybody claims that the situation is important, but then goes their own way. Particular attention is paid to protecting one's own position and making use of all the possibilities that the organization, despite everything, may still offer. The symptoms are similar to those caused by AIDS: the immune system is attacked and the self-healing and self-regenerating abilities of the organization are destroyed. The result is a culture that stays stuck in a rut. People loose their enthusiasm and remain constrained in a box with no room for modern forms of cooperation and creative solutions to problems.

When the Entitlement Culture rules, it is increasingly difficult to deal with change. The following problems are connected with this way of treating each other:

- Fear of making decisions
- Politically correct behavior; little passion and energy
- Work performances cannot easily be discussed
- Many external attributes; lack of taking responsibility for one's own problems
- Too much emphasis placed on hierarchy and function, it becomes very difficult to bring a project to a good completion
- Planned change becomes changed plans
- Insufficient attention to market and customers
- Ability to change is blocked

Any organization that no longer develops, robs its employees of the chance to develop themselves and is thus for the well-being of those

CULTURAL DEVELOPMENT

ENTITLEMENT CULTURE		ADDED VALUE CULTURE
Who is authorized to do what?	→	What is the added value from the contribution?
Whose fault is it?	→	How do we come to a solution?
Focused on the past	→	Focused on the present and future
Everyone treated equally	→	The more you achieve, the more you earn
What are my rights?	→	What can I contribute?
Overly cautious	→	Confrontation in a business like manner

directly involved a 'criminal organization'. Those employees who are prepared to change, gradually leave the organization, which over exaggerates the stagnation of those left behind. The result is a very destructive and self-fulfilling spiral in which it is increasingly difficult to bring about change.

RADICAL CHANGE OR SLOW DEATH

> *"First we shape our structure, then our structures shape us."*
> – Winston Churchill

The big problem with a (rigid) Entitlement Culture is that the collective has stopped developing itself and is not open to any influences from outside. People then get trapped in "more of the same" and are insufficiently aware that because of this the problems only get harder to solve. Sometimes the chosen solutions even worsen the problem. The fact that people keep searching in the wrong place has nothing to do with the intelligence or motivation of the people who suggest the solutions. The real problem is that once again people have too little connection to the current era and its dynamic for change. And so people approach reality with dated ideas and the behavior associated with them. This means that people are ever running after the facts and trying to deal with the restrictions of the adopted thinking. This behavior mechanism takes its toll of course and ultimately causes people to become discouraged and disillusioned and decide not to expend what is left of their energy on supra-personal aims.

It is high time that we become aware of the way we approach social and organizational reality. The spectacles we wear greatly affect what we see, do, and experience. It is all about the following process of transformation of awareness:*

TRANSFORMATION OF AWARENESS

The world is	The world will become
Know your place	Create your own space
External control	Internal control
Hierarchy	Accountability
Tour	Expedition

Stability, predictability, and regularity no longer determine the picture of social reality. Times are changing whether some people like it or not. If a deliberate change process is added, then the picture can become chaotic, diffuse, and uncontrollable. It is not surprising that many feel abandoned or even betrayed by employers who are unable in the current time warp to keep the promises made in the industrial awareness era. But employers too can feel powerless be-

* Inspired by André Wierdsma.

cause of the rapid changes that make old psychological contracts (security in exchange for loyalty) no longer able to be honored.

If the world is changing too fast for your liking, then you must find security and grounding in yourself. For this you must at least allow yourself to entertain the thought that the world has changed, there is no going back, and that these circumstances demand a change in mentality and awareness. Our ultimate challenge is to change radically or to die slowly.

STIFFS OR LIVING ORGANISMS

> *"They get you to stand under a waterfall with a bucket and tell you: catch the water."*

When people try to explain an organization to you, they usually do this using an organizational chart and the associated function descriptions. This paper reality clearly shows who is responsible for what and who reports to whom. This custom shows how attached we are to graphs and tables and to the suggestion that we have everything under control. Yet everybody knows that the organizational reality is much more complex. Because such a chart will never show who finds who sympathetic, nor will it show the informal lines of command. And yet human chemistry still provides the best explanation of why a department works well. And so an organizational chart is best compared to a map of the countryside; reality is reduced to a two-dimensional representation, but you only get to know what the area looks like when you are at the spot yourself.

This love of charts can best be explained by the feeling one gets through tables and graphs that there is actually somebody in control and that the most important processes take place in an orderly fashion. But as we have already said, reality is much more complex and disorganized. That is why it is important to decide from which awareness level you should approach reality. It makes a big difference if you approach an organization as a machine or as a living organism:*

ORGANIZATION AS MACHINE

Environment	– *well organized* – *predictable*
Organization	– *sum of parts* – *management almighty, all-knowing*
Themes	– *order (control & monitoring)* – *risks (limit as much as possible)*
Change	– *package tour*
Invitation	– *would you be so kind as to follow me?*

The *machine* model was most appropriate in the industrial era, when there was more or less a stable environment. In this philosophy, organizational problems were largely solved through reorganization (restructuring/acquisition). Aims were formulated by management and plans for change were drawn up that were intended to lead the organization step by step to the desired goal. The journey goes from A to B, with a number of intermediate steps and a final goal in mind. To neutralize the worst insecurities among the workforce, protocols were often laid down and agreements reached about employment. People spoke of a "change project." The promise was that, after the reorganization, a new period of stability would set in. The underlying psychological contract with the employees was: "*Trust me: I am a good shepherd and will lead you to new green pastures.*"

The *living organism* model suits a social reality that is characterized by turbulence and unpredictability. In this philosophy, organizations must be capable of reacting to this and of achieving the tempo of change demanded of them. Change is a constant factor and thus the organization will be constantly on the move. The jour-

* As depicted by André Wierdsma.

Environment	– *dynamic* – *unpredictable*
Organization	– *processes and relationships* – *realization of goals, connection*
Themes	– *self-organization and accountability* – *co-creation of a sense of meaning*
Change	– *adventurour journey in the direction of collective ambitions*
Invitation	– *how can we work together to bring this ambition to life?*

ney goes from A to "somewhere else" and is intended to allow the individual and the organization to grow to its full potential. Nobody thinks they know best nor does anybody try to give believable guarantees for the future. Everybody must learn to live with insecurity. We live with increasing insight and the organization is recreated every day afresh. This is only possible if everybody accepts their own responsibility. The psychological contract with the employees is: *"Together we will create an organization of which we can all be proud."*

TOUR GROUP AND BACKPACKER

"Life is not just a journey of discovery, it is a process of creation."

Change activities are generally greeted with reticence or even revulsion. This resistance to change is not natural, because very few people get enthusiastic about doing the same thing for the next 20 years. A standard complaint is that the work is dull and doesn't offer any challenge. Looked at in this light, any change should be warmly welcomed. And yet in practice people prefer the existing discomfort to the challenging prospect of improvement. It is a strategy rooted in poverty: it is born out of a deep feeling of dependency and a distrust of management's true intentions. This distrust has major consequences for all involved. If distrust gets the upper hand, then no decisions can be made smoothly. Everything is endlessly discussed and people constantly question each other's motives. Everybody is constantly in a bind and tries to find some security in procedures and guarantees. What's more, people are for ever trying to prove that they are worthy of the trust they have not yet been given. The result is a no-win race.

A change process makes enormous demands on people and on the underlying relationships of trust. It is therefore vital that any problems of trust are discussed and, where possible, resolved. Distrust causes feelings of insecurity and paralysis. But unexpressed distrust is even worse and ultimately castrates any form of cooperation. Without trust in each other's intentions and capacities, people would be better not to set out on a journey.

If people have agreed on the need and direction of the development process and trust each other's intentions, then there is a basis for setting off on a journey together. The question remains: tour or expedition? People on a tour approach change processes differently than those on an expedition. The following model clarifies the differences in the various change dimensions:*

	TOUR	EXPEDITION
Goal	➤ Arrival	➤ Vitality and market oriented
Result	➤ Structural change	➤ Mindset/essence
Starting point	➤ Top down	➤ Trust the process
Strategy	➤ Blueprint	➤ Advancing insight
Motivation	➤ Duty	➤ Energy
Approach	➤ Organization-wide	➤ Core group
Management-direction	➤ Content / Power & Procedures	➤ Process / Inspiration & Success

* The model is inspired by Joop Swieringa and Bianca Ebbers.

The *tourgroup* knows the destination and organizes the journey so that they can reach that destination as efficiently as possible. When planning the journey, they do not bother about unexpected circumstances. For the tourgroup, the world during the trip remains static and they only adapt to unplanned eventualities with reluctance.

The *backpacker* also decides in advance the direction the expedition will take him and his final goal. He prepares himself as well as possible, but knows that during his expedition unexpected things will happen – both pleasant and unpleasant. If, during the expedition, he makes new discoveries or develops new attitudes, then he changes his destination or adapts the change strategy. He enjoys the journey and confidently follows his own path.

Where one group yearns for security and predictability, the other looks forward to adventure and excitement. Naturally the chosen approach depends on the social and organizational perspective from which it is stems. The 'tourgroup' generally regards the organization (and their social environment) as a machine; the backpacker generally considers the organization (and his social environment) as a living organism.

Because of the current fast paced "communication era," the change specialist will generally favor the side of the backpacker. After all, in a jungle a compass is of more use than a roadmap and improvisational talent better than a rigid adherence to the prescribed route. Although the exact need not be mapped out, it is essential to know the extent of change that everybody is aiming for and whether this is appropriate for the situation at hand. This should be agreed to in advance because if, during the journey, you are going to stop and discuss everything, this will discourage involvement and perhaps even encourage some to get off the train altogether.

CHANGING FROM THE INSIDE

> *"The problem is not how to discover new ideas, but how to escape from the old ones"* – John Maynard Keynes

When people start to see the organization as a living organism, assumptions from the industrial and machine era lose their validity. The greatest assumption is that change must be thought up, managed, initiated, and controlled by the top. This implies that the top must know exactly where they are going and know better than the employees the way things are progressing. A leader is like a general at the head of an army: "I attack, follow me."

This idea of leadership and dependence on the leader is no longer applicable when we think of an organization as a living organism. Changes take place so quickly that nobody can permit themselves any longer to pretend that the world isn't changing. Thinking up and implementing improvements and revitalizations is something everybody has to do. And thus everybody deserves an invitation to this process of creation. It is all about "changing from the inside" and "many changing much."

Changing from the inside requires five creative abilities:

- *Imagination* (people are able to use their fantasy and imagine the desired situation)
- *Creative ability* (people are predestined to test and dispute borders; this is certainly true of borders that cause unrest)
- *The desire for partnership and comradeship* (people desire closeness and prefer not to be alone in going for change)
- *Commitment* (people feel most responsible for realizing solutions that they have thought up themselves)
- *Sense of community* (people have the ability to place personal interests in a supra-personal context and where necessary make sacrifices for the collective).

"Changing from the inside" means mobilizing and using these qualities. The following ideas can be inspirational in designing change processes:

- *Make a picture of the organizational reality you desire; define the collective ambition level and the rules of behavior associated with it.* For this, we need to make (or re-establish) contact with our dreams and ideals about the functioning of the organization and its environment. The challenge is to develop a proposition that is *different* to the existing possibilities. Not *just as good*, because then you descend to copying others and the consumer makes a choice simply based on price. The result is price erosion and then everybody is in a mess. Not *better*, because that only provides a temporary advantage. You only have a winning strategy if you offer something that your competitor cannot offer. Just like the Ritz Carlton hotel group with its mystique (create exceptional memories) and Lexus with its red-carpet treatment of its clients. What's more, it is exceptionally exciting and challenging to create a special proposition with your colleagues and to develop it and get it to market.
- *Self-assessment of alignment and team spirit.* It is vital that the people responsible should assess deeply and thoroughly what reality they desire and whether they are fully committed to the defined strategies. If there is only the slightest hint of doubt or lack of cooperation at the top, then it will be difficult to free the necessary forces for the revitalization project. The top is often faced with a difficult task. They must help the organization give shape both internally and externally to the desired change, while remaining responsible for the situation as it currently exists. People have to move out of their own shadow, and this demands enthusiasm, persuasion, vitality, trust and passion. Without these, at times of adversity, good intentions can wither into distrust, grumbling, and egocentricity.
- *Focus on the existing quality, energy, and readiness to change.* Healthy people and organizations are exceptionally capable of "re-inventing themselves" and providing the extra exertion this requires. It is important to harness and leverage this capacity. Hiring out-

siders and making external forces overly responsible for the change process only reinforces the idea that change is a matter for people outside the organization. This robs people of the chance of learning and increases the feeling of helplessness. What's more, it increases the danger that any revitalization that is implemented is foreign to the organization itself and is rejected by it.

■ *Board of inspiration.* In their infancy, change processes are vulnerable things. Everybody has an opinion about them and massive resistance – either open or hidden – can exist against them. It is vital, therefore, to organize sufficient acceptance and support. This can be done by bringing together all formal and informal leaders in a Board of Inspiration. This group will act as the "spider in the web," and help by establishing cross-links (management, governors, trade union representatives, customers, and employees), and, where necessary, protect the whole process from more conservative forces. It is crucial that the Board of Inspiration does not act as a substitute for existing management systems who are responsible for making sure routine activities continue to take place. The 'Board' is primarily about feeding, creating and where necessary protecting the revitalization processes.

■ *Get on board.* Getting people involved in the change process means first and foremost directing your energies at those people in the environment who think positively about the process. These opinion makers can, through training sessions, be given the necessary flexibility and change qualities. In addition, it is important to organize networks, which offer social support and stimulate learning through experience. The enthusiasm of the beginners gradually infects their colleagues. They are then also invited to take a leading role. And so, slowly but surely, a growing group of change agents is formed, whose members together provide an increasing amount of energy for change and inspiration.

■ *Concentrate on doing what you can do in your immediate surroundings.* Remember real changes come down to the individual and the relationships maintained with the immediate surroundings. An individual can only exert significant influence over large matters indirectly or with the help of other individuals. That is why it is important, wherever possible, to make the area of change as narrow as possible and to reduce it to human proportions. If the themes are made too wide and have to be studied within their context and in combination with each other, then paralysis can arise. It can become too big to handle. Start small and keep it manageable.

■ *Encourage communication.* A new awareness can be achieved and nurtured by a constant and consistent flow of information. It is all about allowing people to acknowledge the problems in the current situation and to create new ideas of their own. Small information and communication meetings in the direct work environment are much more effective than large-scale meetings. The contributions made by colleagues (peer pressure) often have greater influence than that exerted by external professionals or top management.

■ *During the process, be consistent about the chosen starting-points.* People will start believing in the process if they notice that they are being approached in a consistent and genuine manner. Efforts must be made to prevent the old bureaucratic patterns of behavior re-establishing itself during the change process. Otherwise, before you know it, there are once again project bureaus, independent change managers, and job descriptions, and everything that lives and moves is castrated by dead letters and masked fear of change. Right from the start, high demands are made of the behavior and self-critical mind of leading functionaries.

■ *Light-footed management.* If, in this new thinking, collective ambition and mutual agreement about aims decides the boundaries, then it is advisable to give these regulatory mechanisms the free hand. Do not tie up a process in advance with all sorts of protocols and procedures. But make sure existing agreements are met under the motto: we apply a minimum of rules.

Changing from the inside places enormous demands on the courage of internal corporate administrators to differentiate and manifest themselves. In many corporate cultures, this is not without danger. You are soon seen as a show-off or somebody who's trying to make a career for themselves in some underhanded way. You not only have to work on your own individual flexibility, but also build up a social network. The motto is: "You must give form to your own life, but you don't need to do it alone."

MISSION, PRINCIPLES, AND PERFORMANCE

"Pretty words only magnify existing cynicism and sarcasm."

What is more attractive than an organization that does what it says? Or perhaps does even more. It generates pride and a positive identification and improves the performance of the organization as a whole. Nothing works as potently as success. But for that, everybody has to know what the core values and norms of the organization are. And then they need to commit to them. Only then can a winning team of individuals emerge who choose, first and foremost, to let each other function better. This philosophy is at odds with the pattern found in many organizations.

In many organizations, the PR department holds the power. Reality is beautified in an artistic way, which may be all very well for the outside world but can be very demoralizing for those in the organization. The façade is cleaned up without doing anything about the interior. This results in a large difference between the inner and outer worlds, between expectations and results. You can talk of a divided world, in which outer appearances take the place of a healthy sense of reality.

When it is clear what the organization stands for, it develops an enormous attraction. The outside world knows what the organization stands for and the inside world knows "what should be done."

The company manages itself. Being clear on what the underlying values and norms are makes way for a successful, healthy organization. The people inside the organization are assured that everybody shares the same ideas about what the most important value-adding norms and values are. During a change process it is better understood what long-term perspective is served by short-term efforts.

- Everybody knows what the guiding principles are against which individual performance is judged.
- Everybody sees the total plan to which each individual performance contributes. It helps people rise above individual differences and conflicts.

We often see much time being spent communicating and holding meetings. The question is whether all such communication efforts are really necessary. The answer is simple: if everyone is on the same page then there need not be so many meetings. Unfortunately what is often the case is that there is a lack of a communal sense of directive and the shared norms and values (culture). As long as these visionary and cultural mechanisms are lacking, then the organization sentences itself to move from one incident to another. Without a shared ideal, every question, every incident, and every complaint becomes a confrontation with the fact that there is no communal feeling. You cannot force awareness and meaning on people; it is everybody's individual task to develop this and give it content. Only then is there a chance that a communally defined identity can develop and provide direction to organizational units and the people attached to them. A well-founded, accepted, and explicit mission statement is essential. If this is absent, then any attempt to use force or apply a management strategy is doomed to failure. The individual employee retreats from everything that is considered unrealistic or impractical and refuses to see why he should subjugate his own autonomy to the greater whole. On a micro-level, everybody may be working as hard as they can, but any connection with the big picture is missing. When we talk about alignment at an organizational level, then we have to answer the following questions:

- Are the mission statement and corporate strategy the pet project of a top manager or does everybody feel committed to them?
- To what extent do strategy and execution match?
- What influence does the mission statement have on practical matters such as the selection of new employees and their introductory period?
- How is the Human Resource report produced and to what extent do those on the work-floor recognize it?
- Is there an integral approach to organizational development processes (mission/vision, strategy, structure, systems, style of leadership, necessary skills and workforce and the way people treat each other).

If people know what it is all about, they no longer need to be motivated. That is why it is essential to formulate the collective ambition (mission, vision, and strategy) in down-to-earth language. In addition, it is essential that you do not get caught up in one-sided top/down processes. People create meaning together.

ALIGNING INDIVIDUAL AND ORGANIZATION

> *"All mankind is divided into three classes: those who are immovable, those who are movable, and those who move."* – Benjamin Franklin

Often, things are regulated by individual processes. The organization formulates a vision/strategy and the employee asks himself, publicly or privately, just how his own identity can be satisfying linked to that of the organization. There used to be a certain subservience of the individual to the organization, but in certain professional areas that is no longer the case. It is all about a mutual added value. Real talent is not interested in an average organization.

Why should they be? Real talent asks – just like the organization – what profit is there from a temporary or permanent attachment. It is essential that we address such attachment issues:

- Do people find the mission, aims, and the way people treat each other appealing?
- Does one's own principles, values, and norms match the aims of the organization and department?
- Do the people in the organization feel safe, recognized, respected, and invited to contribute to attaining these organizational aims?
- Do individual ideals match those of the organization?
- Do individual expectations about development sufficiently match the possibilities offered by the organization?
- Do the leaders try sufficiently to facilitate and serve and are they prepared to examine their own behavior if it appears that they are part of the problem?

Nothing is more threatening to the credibility and vitality of the change processes than an on-going distinction between wish and reality. Indifference is deadly. It is therefore crucial in any change process to pay sufficient (and on-going) attention to the question about attachment, about whether behavior matches intention.

THE FUNCTIONAL ANARCHIST

> *"I prefer to speak my mind with the chance that I am wrong, rather than silently accepting injustice."*

Anybody who looks critically at organizations will be impressed by the degree of acquiescence with which people continue to follow ridiculous rules and procedures. Anybody looking more carefully is likely to see something else: the creativity and industry with which employees circumvent these rules or turn them to their own advantage. This anarchy – depending on which view you take – has a positive and a less positive side.

In many companies, anarchy is essential. If every single rule is followed, then a company, thanks to its decision-making rituals, will often be "a day late and a dollar short." On the other hand, if everybody does his own thing, then the necessary communal direction will be missing. The key is flexibility and collaborative effort. If it has not been clearly stated which strategies will be chosen and why, how can management really expect the employees to embrace them. When there is a lack of straight forward communication, then people feel ignored and have the natural tendency to go their own way. Furthermore, as mentioned above, when rules are set from the top down and required to be strictly followed then the natural human creativity is suppressed. This tends to lead to subversion. Only built in flexibility will allow people the latitude to participate toward the greater good, while feeling that they are making their own unique contribution. As a result, there will be added value for the necessary change processes.

COMPLAINT TO MANAGEMENT	ANTIDOTE
There is no strategy here	What contribution can I make?
The are no clear aims	I know what I want and am full of initiative and enterprise
The structure is unclear	Functions here are allocated just for form
On paper, everything is top-down	On the shop-floor, there is room for own initiative
Imagination has no say here	Everybody is creative and thinks, decides, and does
We never see them	Good thing, now we can do what we like
They are serious and self-important	What about a little humor and putting things in perspective
I never get a chance	I present my own plans and ideals, if necessary to another employer

The assignment for the functional anarchist is to put forward his opinion. He should say what he stands for instead of simply criticizing and complaining about what others have suggested. Come up with solutions. If the rules or strategies don't make sense, then think of other ways to make things work. If you do not take control, you will be controlled. Make a contribution.

NO NONSENSE WITH A HEART

"A river without banks is a mud pool." – Ken Blanchard

Progress often occurs thanks to idealism, daring, and optimism. It means having the courage to leave the well-worn paths and to think up and implement unorthodox solutions. You do this by following your ideals and your inner drive and by continuing regardless of your own successes or failures. You believe in yourself, in your vision, and in the future, and believe there is always room for improvement. It also means pressing on when others stop, because things have become too difficult, demand too much exertion, or encounter too much opposition. Real progression is about taking risks, going beyond the imposed limits and, if there is no other choice, even putting your job on the line. With bold action, often comes serious consequences but also enormous prospects.

Initiating or accelerating change is neither mild nor non-committal. It causes tension but also satisfaction, it takes you to the very limit of your patience. It reveals what you stand for and what you are worth when it really comes down to it. A few points deserve special mention:

- Choosing for change may be risky; not choosing may be even more risky. It is true for everybody that the quality of life depends on the quality of the choices made. In practice, "not choosing" means throwing in the towel and making your happiness dependent on decisions made by others. In other words: "If you do not control yourself, others will control you."

- If a relationship has no added value for the people concerned, then the relationship is out of balance. A continued imbalance will cause displeasure and probably digress further, causing more intense negative emotions; reason enough for all parties involved to make the relationship more vital so that everybody experiences some added value through continuing it.
- If the relationship has ended up in a permanent imbalance, if it has gone so far that it is unable to be saved, then it is best for everybody to move on and leave behind the illusion that things will improve. But frequently the courage to do this isn't there. Starting a relationship proves, in practice, easier than ending one. This inconvenience is frequently elevated to "social policy," but is, despite all good intentions, frequently the cause of stress or burn-out. It is better for everybody to end the relationship if you no longer feel able to warmly embrace the other person (or organization) and if a change for the better has become highly unlikely.

If change is to be successful, then reality must be preferred to public relations. It is not wise in the long run to carry on pulling the wool over everybody's eyes.

Honesty: The Best Policy means, in this context, clearly and respectfully combining attitudes and behavior that at first sight may seem rather incompatible:

– Ensuring room for development	– Expecting added value
– Giving space	– Setting limits
– Looking after someone	– Making demands
– Comradeship	– Business-like
– Caring for someone	– Dismissing someone in time.

What we need to do is simultaneously channel and make room for unique human qualities. This principle is called "guided autonomy," freedom within limits. A difficult concept, since at first glance it seems to be dealing with contradictory forces.

It is sometimes difficult to make clear in a working relationship that both mobilizing and supporting qualities play a simultaneous role. They are two sides of the same coin. Without a clearly articulated business and demanding dimension, the relational and supporting dimension has no solid base. That is why in our own creed about managing people we use the term: "No-Nonsense with a Heart."

The shift towards added value and self-determination thinking demands a personal and organizational transformation. Without such changes, too much energy is wasted on rationalizing existing routines and maintaining role patterns from the past. Then disappointment is inevitable and *suspicion*, *cynicism* and *powerlessness* gain the upper hand. Choosing for change is a synonym for choosing for hope, love, and meaningful change. Your standpoint should be formed by your own ideals and your own image of reality, not whether they can be achieved or whether they are politically correct. When we are true to ourselves then we find, to our ultimate benefit, that Honesty IS the Best Policy.

6

TORTOISES AND HARES

"Philosophers have explained the world, now it's time to change it."
– Ludwig Feuerbach

THE CURRENT HECTIC and chaotic times cause unrest, uncertainty, and feelings of insecurity. We continuously ask ourselves what is hanging above our heads. Some take advantage of the situation and dive into opportunism or unethical behavior. Other people choose victim-like behavior and believe they are the brunt of all adversity. Both reactions are directed at short-term individual survival and are thus, at their heart, egocentric and indolent. Dishonesty is often a logical by-product of this.

It is, none the less, an exceptionally interesting time for our inner social architect and the artist. Full of dynamic, tension, and unimagined opportunities. Because where there is such movement, there are new possibilities for market, product, and personal development. It is important to retain your basic trust in the developments and consider yourself an active participant in their design. You always feel better if you are the one who has the next move and have some active influence on the game. That is why it is more important than ever to use your inner strength and conviction and to call on and develop your inborn ability for self-determination. It causes a transformation from a life that was previously ruled by external expectations to a life that is developed, strengthened, and directed from inside. You no longer live according to the wishes of others, but instead set your own priorities and feel responsibility for what you do.

It is essential that you make it very clear to yourself what you stand for and what your ambitions are, so that you can design and construct your own reality and look the world in the eye. Each change therefore demands a high level of ego-searching: it means looking for inner evidence, rather than satisfying external demands and expectations. But how do we discover what our inner sources of wisdom are?

■ First of all, by admitting to ourselves that conditioning and socialization influences have estranged us from ourselves and led us astray. These influences have, naturally, brought us, at least superficially, a lot of good. But so-called "free choices" can only be really free if we were fully aware of the context and meaning of these choices. For the rest, our behavior is driven mainly by the complex pressures exerted by culture which we, as individuals, experience. This can be the pressure of a particular social context, corporate culture, language, morals or habits; in short, things that we obey without being conscious of them. If you live in Eire, then you are automatically catholic; if you live in Northern Ireland, then you are assumed to be protestant. If we are to increase the psychological space for real personal and sovereign choices, we have to become much more aware of the mental programming that drives our behavior. In other words: we have to become more aware of the spectacles we put on when we look at and judge the world and ourselves. If too little attention is given to this awareness process, then there is every chance that we will continue repeating our old patterns and problems. Even if we feel unhappy in such a situation.

■ Take time for regular reflection and introspection. Sufficient inner peace is the only means for creative growth and radical change. It is hardly surprising that our best ideas and breakthroughs come at times when we are not looking for them; under the shower, at a traffic light, or walking in a forest. We are open to things that come unannounced. The eagerness of the intellect has, at such moments, no control over us. There is, of course, nothing wrong with using "common sense." There is everything against a one-sided rational approach to reality, since this closes the mind to a more comprehensive and intuitive approach to the problem.

The most important element in self-determination is managing the factor "time." Because how can we discover what we want to create if we allow one activity to blend into the next? Do we move from incident to incident? And thus allow ourselves to be guided by circumstances? Perhaps one of the most serious and prevalent mistakes we make is to think we have to approach the current turbulence at top speed. For speed demands speed and "standing still means falling behind." Can we really solve external chaos and insecurity by attacking it with inner chaos and estrangement? Nothing is more unsuitable for personal and organizational development than adopting without criticism the rhythm of the times. And this is particularly true if that rhythm does not match the tempo of the processes within the individual.

In his books, philosopher Arnold Cornelis describes three realities that, for a healthy development, must constantly be kept in tune with each other:

- The external clock (the constantly increasing demands from our environment)
- The internal clock (do the movements/challenges match the person's internal program and can they be integrated into it?)
- The psychological reality (how does someone experience his or her situation, and are they happy with it?).

When these three realities become separated from each other and are not approached in a cohesive way, then they can become a source of stress. The core question in any developmental situation is: may I develop my underlying desires own essence and the associated possibilities? If we are to prevent ourselves from spinning out of control, then it is vital that, as the speed of the external clock accelerates, the speed of the internal clock decelerates. That means taking more time for reflection, and reserving more time for experiencing and processing events. That means pausing and being open to things that present themselves. Otherwise the internal clock will turn like mad in "more of the same" processes and the estrangement factors associated with this. It is precisely in rapidly changing circumstances that we should keep in touch with our psychological reality and allow our unique inner program to see, value, and develop. Then you will be fit, motivated, and see the possibilities of whatever presents itself from your own strength. In this sense, we mustn't allow others to "persuade" us but rather always rely on our own inner psychological reality. For ultimately, the motivation for change is derived from the question of whether the person's essence underlying desires will benefit from it.

Unfortunately, we have come to look on happiness as the total realization of all our individual ecstatic dreams. Everything has to step aside for this, and we are even prepared to risk our health and morality. Real happiness is rooted in a quiet contemplation of reality and finding peace in this. That is why we must never think that reality is better than it is. At a given moment, we have to know, accept, and demonstrate exactly who we are and no longer acquiesce by being and doing what other people expect of us. Thus the psychological reality is that "we must regularly stand still in order to move forward." All estrangement and stress that we feel now is the result of an inability to sit still, to be alone, and to make decisions for and by ourselves about the contribution we will make now and in the future.

CREATE SPACE FOR PLOTTING OUR COURSE

"Everyone is a natural talent, as long as you give nature the space."

All real change comes from the inside and is the result of a person's internal program (essence), dreams, desires, capacities, and talents.

It is thus important to maintain (or re-establish) in the "here-and-now" contact with our ideals, drives, and sources of motivation. If we are to clarify these sources of inspiration, then it is best that we start close to ourselves. Perhaps the following questions will help in this self-analysis:*

About yourself:

- Who am I, when am I at my full strength?
- What is most real about myself?
- Why is it sometimes better not to be the real me?
- What is my unique added value for others?
- What gives me energy, what costs energy?
- What do I keep hidden from myself (and thus from others)? What pattern do I use to do this?
- What happened to the vitality and uniqueness of my childhood?
- What do I live for? What am I most passionate about?
- What can stop me doing what my heart tells me to do?

About work:

- What are my ambitions and desires in my work?
- Why is this work important to me?
- Why is it important to me to be a leader/professional?
- What would I do if I were financially independent?
- What will I need to discover about myself in order to find passionate work?
- What do I want to achieve in my direct surroundings?
- What am I most afraid of in my work?

You do not need to do this exercise alone. A partner can help by posing the questions. The task for the partner is that they restrict themselves to giving attention, and unselfish, non-controlling support.

* Inspired by the book *The Diamond Approach* by John Davis

Expressing opinions or making judgments will only narrow the self-analysis to an exchange of experiences or even a debate about "which one is right."

The thinking behind this self-analysis is that when we get to know ourselves better, obstructions will be removed, the internal program will develop itself, and higher possibilities for development will present themselves. This idea of change is diametrically opposed to the current idea that change activities begin by defining the desired future. We must make two remarks here:

- Excessive concentration on thinking and defining the future scenario only masks the existing discomfort about the responsibilities we face today. The focus must be sufficiently directed at clarifying and understanding the problematic reality of here and now. This will prevent us from setting out to a projected future with too much optimism and without sufficient grounding.
- Although every sports club starts a new season by setting its ambition level, condition training, and team-building activities, such a thing is far from usual in a company. Many projects are simply started with a pep-talk and the participants then have to get on with it together. There is little or no explicit attention given to the chemistry between those involved and whether they even know each other's "whys." And yet it is important for any collective to understand in advance the ambition level, drives, and qualities of those involved (the "whys" of the individuals). In addition to learning about individual themes and awareness, it is sensible to discuss the collective's awareness level.

About the collective in which we operate:

- Who are we and what binds us together?
- What responsibilities do we have for the current situation?
- What organizational reality do we wish to create together?
- Why is it important for our company/department to reach full development?

- What would convince the others that each of us is suitable for the change process being considered?
- What should we discover about our work and our relationship to it?
- What can we do to alleviate the existing pain and resistance to change that surrounds us?

Defining the level of ambition is, in practice largely a cognitative process. It leads to wonderful but empty sentences that reveal a great gap between wish and reality. Thanks to this, a process is corrupted right at the very start and small steps in the right direction are insufficient and sometimes even suspect. Each sentence and resolution needs to be accompanied by a question: do we really mean what it says or is this political language? In the latter case, there is no sincere intention to change; the existing reality will most likely continue or get worse.

MAKE OPTIMAL USE OF THOUGHT AND ENERGY

"We can no longer permit ourselves to suffer unnecessary loss of energy."

When we strive to build a better future for ourselves and our children, we encounter the full extent of human imperfection and potential perfection. It can prove surprising at times that when we look at people who perform adequately and consistently in routine situations, they often choke in a stressful and uncertain situation. And conversely, people who, in the opinion of others, are often trouble makers or unreliable, can suddenly emerge as leaders and sources of inspiration. Change processes are, in this light, the litmus test of individual integrity, flexibility, and readiness to make sacrifices. Therefore it is important to recognize:

■ When the pressure is on, then it becomes clear how people really relate to themselves and their surroundings. The core values tend to emerge.

■ It is not sensible to hold on to the concept of the way a person functioned in the past.

It is important to enter into change processes with a fresh mind and to keep a watchful eye on what is actually taking place. What's more – and this is the most important – it is essential to break down obstacles in individual and collective functioning. Individual imperfection may have been acceptable in the routine of yesterday, but during a change process the motto is: "All hands on deck." Anybody who feels insecure deep inside, will become even more insecure. And anybody who is walking around with pent-up pain and emotions is in even greater danger of feeling powerless with all the depressive feelings associated with it. In short: change activities do not cause extra suffering, but rather place the existing feelings under a magnifying glass. That is why it is so important for the leading people in a change process to develop a genuine and realistic picture of who they are and what they can (potentially) contribute. When leaders are fully secure within themselves they are better equipped to objectively observe and possibly assist others in the transformation process.

In addition, a real understanding of individual hang-ups and restrictions will prevent the process from serious derailment. In this self-analysis, we have to look the following restricting factors in the eye:

Individual obstacles:
- Painful and even traumatic memories and experiences
- Denial symptoms and blind spots
- Unarticulated feelings of insecurity, threat, and other psychological discomfort
- A lack of courage and real independence.

Collective obstacles:
- Unresolved power conflicts within the team
- Distrust between team members
- Dysfunctional cultural behavior pattern (Entitlement Culture)
- Disbelief in changeability.

Any emotional obstacle that is not removed will ultimately come home to roost as an insoluble and repetitive pattern of behavior. Or it will reveal itself as continuous unjust projections and value judgments about the behavior of others. Anybody who really wants to make a difference at an individual level cannot afford to spare himself and must, with or without the help of therapy, gain a full and realistic understanding of his own motives.

EXCEED EXPECTATIONS

> *"Some men see things as they are and say why... I dream of things that never were and say why not."* – Robert F. Kennedy

The expectations of customers and employees are growing spectacularly. With the worldwide market of today and easier migration from one place to the next, not only customers but also employees can easily shop around. It is no longer enough to be just a little bit better than the competitor. In fact, competing is getting harder to maintain as the scope expands. That is why once again we return to the importance of excelling. If a company concentrates on excelling, that is exceeding all expectations and pleasantly surprising its customers and employees, it will result in stronger loyalty. On an individual level, this concept works too. Rather than look to the others and try to "beat them at their own game" (something people with a strong foothold in the rat race are prone to do) you should make up your own game. Find for yourself an authentic approach to your own life, your work and your relationships. Then excel in it. Be the best you can be.

MAINTAIN COOPERATION NETWORKS

> *"Offering a service to another, especially when this is not obligatory, is the interest that is paid for living."* – Peter Block

Organizations are facing growing technological possibilities and explosive customer expectations. The sum of these two forces means that it is necessary for organizations to concentrate on improving their developmental processes. Each member of the organization should be on the same page; all carrying out their own assignments to their utmost ability and striving for the highest quality attainable. The people within an organization should think and act metaphorically like a chain, making sure that all the links in that chain are working together. If we take the example of a hospital, this point can be illustrated. It is of no real use developing crisis help if the start of the chain, namely admission to the hospital, is not developed as well, equally important would be the follow up or after care for the patient. Naturally the crisis help would meet a vital need of the patient but he would be far better served if all the links worked well together and there was an efficient admission process and good quality care after the crises to insure a complete transition back to full health.

In any attempt to process improvement, it soon becomes clear how common it is to approach reality from existing hierarchical or functional relationships. Organizational change has long been synonymous with functional (sub) optimizing. It demands a major change in culture and awareness for all participants to relate "quality improvement" to process improvement and chain management dependency. And on an individual level, this means developing a sensitivity to processes and actively contributing to the best possible functioning of the total chain, rather than throwing your part of the product into the mix and then waiting to see what happens to it.

LEARN TO ENJOY TRANSITION

"Organizational changes cannot be managed, at best they can be recognized. It is high time that we learned that the control dogma must be relinquished and that we must embrace a certain need for chaos and change dynamics." – André Wierdsma

Much has changed over the years in the relationship between companies and employees. Perhaps the most important change is that only very few employees now assume that they will still be at the same company when it is time to retire. The old barter relationship – we guarantee security in exchange for your loyalty – is in tatters, not least because no company can guarantee under the current circumstances that it will be able to keep its side of the bargain. It is therefore impossible and even unfair for a company to make false promises.

The psychological contract between company and employee has changed enormously and, in a certain sense, has become more realistic. Not everybody is aware of this change or is equipped to rely fully on themselves. And yet it is the reality that a company has, at its core, an economic and social function. Protecting the employee is one of the aims, but not the primary one. So it is essential that we psychologically stand on our own two feet and learn to derive pleasure from the turbulent situation around us. For in a certain sense, everybody is just an interim manager; the viability and with it the underlying reason for an employment contract disappears once the parties no longer experience any added value in the relationship.

ADMIT YOUR DESIRES AND VISION

"The greatest way to live with honour in this world is to be what we pretend to be." – Socrates

In this way of thinking, you are not motivated by what works (pragmatic) or what used to work, but rather by the motives that what you believe in really matters: your idealism, maintaining and extending your relationships, your desire for depth and intimacy. Because not knowing what you stand for or not listening to your conscience leads, by definition, to opportunistic behavior and dishonesty. Next it is important that you accurately give shape to your intentions through adequate behavior. In other words: communicate in accordance with your ideas and viewpoints. You should be clear and transparent, but also in tune with your surroundings. Be unambiguous and convincing, yet committed and inviting. It is important to train yourself in this, because by perfecting your emotional intelligence and presentation techniques, you will avoid unnecessary interference and complexity. Everybody is potentially capable of controlling themselves and being in top emotional condition. The key to maturity is emotional self-determination; and this boils down to taking responsibility for your emotions.

HAVE THE COURAGE AND DISCIPLINE TO GO AGAINST THE TIDE

"The highest form of human happiness is connected to struggle and the defeat of difficulties and danger." – Aristotle

Man is a complete creation with a broad range of emotions. Some emotions are particularly beautiful and positive, others less so. It is a characteristic of existence that high points can only exist thanks to low points. A constant feeling of happiness is simply not possible, not matter how much we may desire it. You will occasionally feel very sad and very alone. The latter will certainly be the case if you occupy yourself with designing and accelerating change. A prophet is never honored in his own country. This is because those who dare to profile themselves clearly and say what is on their minds remind, even unintentionally, those who do not do this that their own courage to come out for what they think is lacking. Instead of recognizing this as a challenge, many choose self-deception and self-pity. You may at times feel alone, but at least you will be faithful to yourself. Courage often entails losing your sense of security for a while. But losing your courage means losing yourself forever.

7

HONESTY: THE BEST POLICY A PERSONAL PERSPECTIVE

"Pain as fuel for passion."

PEOPLE OFTEN SAY that the more fanatical the missionary, the greater the doubt he has in his own message. So am I trying, with this passionate appeal to my readers, to wipe away my own doubts? Or should they become exactly like me, feel like me and think like me? As I wrote this book, this question sometimes presented itself as a paradox. I do not want my readers to become like me. And it is not my aim to have everyone echo the words shouted in chorus in Monty Python's *Life of Brian*: "We are all individuals." My message, rather, is an appeal to the readers to go in search of their own true selves. This book hopefully offers some thought-provoking remarks and practical tips.

When discussing a subject like "Honesty: The Best Policy," it is important that the reader gets to know something about the author. After all, it is not self-evident why we invest so much time in such a weighty subject. There has to be a deeper motive here to justify the exertions. And so I would like here to raise the veil just a little on my personal background, motives, doubts, and imperfections. Hopefully this will invite you to contemplate again your own story. It is important to remember that only sufficient self-knowledge and self-appreciate can prevent you from treating yourself poorly and going down the path that leads to dishonesty.

MOTIVATION FOR WRITING THIS BOOK

You don't start writing a book unless there is a particular drive to do so. Superficially, the reason for writing this book can be found in my love for my profession. Every training and meeting provides new insights that can be shared with our readers, colleagues, and clients. And that is true. I often think that I have the finest profession in the world. I feel so strongly about what I do that I want to shout from the roof-tops that within companies everything should and must be done differently. There is too much sorrow around, too much unresolved suffering, cynicism, and loneliness. And I, too, often feel so very much alone and rejected.

But without a healthy (or unhealthy) dose of ambition, perseverance, and discipline, a book would never be completed. It is a far too time-consuming process and there are thousands of reasons to give up halfway through. So there is obviously a deep-rooted need to prove myself, to distinguish myself from others, and possibly to gain some applause. Otherwise I would have stopped long ago and would have chosen for other, less exhausting activities. But my inner drive to finish this project always won over my laziness and my easily activated feeling of victimization.

SO THAT OTHERS DO NOT HAVE TO SUFFER THE SAME PAIN

I do not have the pretension that I am *always* completely honest. There are too many moments when, either consciously or sub-consciously, I did not have the courage or the discipline to do something productive with the feelings I had in my heart. Sometimes my feelings of wanting to present myself in a better light than I deserve caused me to choose to play a double role. There is enough about my life (with the awareness that I now have) to cause me shame.

I am by no means perfect and I still hope to learn a lot. In some ways this is a comforting and supporting feeling and an invitation to develop further.

I feel deeply that *honesty is the best policy* because I have been powerfully hurt by people that I loved and trusted not being honest. I had an older sister whose existence I only learned about after the death of my mother and the discovery of a birth certificate. She had died several months after her birth, before I was born. When I asked my father about this, he told me that he and my mother had decided not to tell their children about the death of their first child. It was both a good intention and an impossibility. I became an expert at a young age in hidden pain and unexpressed sorrow; it was something you felt but weren't allowed to know about. Because this is "better for you." I still have difficulties with people who do not deal with information truthfully; and certainly when somebody assumes that the other person won't be able to deal with it.

Now it is my move. I can now add something of myself to the rational analytical qualities of my mother and the emotional spiritual qualities of my father. And it is my job to prevent painful patterns of the past from repeating themselves in the future.

ONCE A CONSCIENTIOUS OBJECTOR, ALWAYS A CONSCIENTIOUS OBJECTOR

I am a conscientious objector. Not from any pacifist or political motives, but purely personal. I believed from a very early age that the army would not elevate me, nor that I would elevate the army. But my most important motive was my resistance to organized violence and the herd mentality this requires. I am still proud that I made a clear choice at the time. However, my choice did not fit the life philosophy of my parents. Deep down, my father wanted to agree with me, but, together with my mother, the fear of the consequences got the upper hand. Would you ever get a good job if they knew you were a conscientious objector? In retrospect, it is one of the best decisions I have ever made. I learned early on to live with the loneliness of existence and with the consequences of independent choices.

Although this decision presented some hardships at the time, in the long term, this experience helped me. It gave me insight into making tough decisions and as a result, allows me to talk about people who think that not choosing is not a choice in itself. What's more, my alternative national service set me on the path to the work I do now.

ALL THE SPACE IN THE WORLD

In the past, I was never, with very few exceptions, particularly impressed by the teachers and managers I had. They seemed mainly interested in obediently following the instructions of those higher up. It became obvious that leadership meant mainly "reassigning pressure" and "laying blame." And yet those in charge, from high to low, were pleasant people, solid, and loyal. However, they were apparently prepared to offer up something of themselves to please those above them. These personality characteristics were welcomed by their "superiors" and admittedly they could also be advantageous to the employees. At times they would seem to allow just about anything as long as they didn't have to devote too much personal attention to it . I was never called to task about the way I did my job, even though I personally thought I should have been. I learned that you really have to make a mess of things before anybody takes any corrective action. In other words: my leaders never had, as people, natural authority, real independence, or personal impact. They were largely concerned with themselves and their endless meetings. I quite liked that though, because it gave me a lot of freedom which only grew when I decided that I had no ambition to make a career for myself.

A MEANINGFUL PATH

Of course I sometimes develop personal feelings when doing my job and leave the offices of clients either feeling pleased that I won't have to spend the rest of my working life there, or I am moved during a training session by the amount of unresolved sorrow and anger. In such a situation, it is not always easy to maintain the necessary distance. But it doesn't help joining the band wagon or making cynical remarks. And so it is important that I keep my mind on the things at hand and keep acting from idealism and compassion. That is not always easy. In organizations, unpleasantness multiplies faster than healing properties. And so organizations seem to suffer from the same inadequacies as individuals. I hope that I will be able, at each moment of integrity, to have the strength and courage to say what I really think and consequently contribute to a situation in which loving forces are in the winning position.

8

CONCLUSION

"Before a child is born, he already knows about oxygen, which is why he is born with lungs not gills. Much knowledge is deep-rooted." – Arnold Cornelis

We must venture back to our authentic self. Get in touch with our inner core. There we will find the answer to the question of how we should approach these ever changing times. Although we have been doing things the same way for a long time and although it seems that we have a long standing infatuation with capitalism and hierarchy, it is important to take a critical look at our well established viewpoints. Many people are discovering that the price they pay for capitalism it is too high. A greedy culture of bartering, revenge, and wheeling and dealing has emerged in which meaningful relationships and the underlying qualities of soul and heart are given less room. In our thirst to climb the hierarchal ladder, more time is spent on corporate politics and matters of survival than on cooperative efforts and building an environment where problems can be solved in a creative and effective way. The result is that we move from one incident to the next, and from one crisis to the next. Nothing seems to last anymore: reputations, financial results, relationships, and moral assumptions all crumble. It clearly shows how deep the pit is and how the current problems are more about society than economy, more about morals than possessions.

It is not easy to wrestle ourselves out of this situation:

- Lately everybody has become accustomed to the prosperity and success that has been fairly cheaply achieved. This has eroded

our natural resilience so that we are defenseless against adversity and insecurity.
- The growth of material prosperity has made a luxurious lifestyle seem so self-evident that many people forget they are responsible for their own fate. We are, in a certain sense, weakened; we have forgotten to stand for something and too often choose the easy way out.

Now the tide is turning, and we are confronted with a more direct relationship between our performance and its results. And then we discover that we have counted ourselves rich and at the same time (or because of this?) we have lost our fighting spirit. It is high time that we win back what we have lost on our journey, so that we can simply act according to our heart and once again stand for things that we feel and mean deeply. Without reserve, without detour, constructively and honestly.

The perceived urgency for change is great; the impotence to do anything with this feeling is equally great. Moreover, the problems we face cannot be solved by legislation or more governmental control. This will simply lead to a greater jungle of rules, even more alienation, and a constant, ever-more ingenious rat race between inspectors and those who try to dodge inspection. The endless search for more instruments, methods, techniques, and skills will, moreover, divert us from accepting our humanity and human limitations. In the fevered search for instruments, we ourselves become what we seek: an instrument.

Two problems must be overcome in order to rid ourselves of feelings of stagnation and powerlessness:

- *The lack of courage to uncover what is really the matter.* Why isn't an organization functioning at its best? Why do policy resolutions end up as empty plans? Why are existing instruments not used to the fullest? And why do those who really want change have to provide a more water-tight case in evidence than somebody who wishes to maintain the existing unsatisfactory situation?

- *The lack of courage to attach consequences to your own opinions or standpoints.* When the chips are down, the heroes turn out to be cardboard cutouts, the memory doesn't function very well anymore and a choice is made, not for the first time, for the easy way out. Thus many managers lose their credibility and many change processes lose their vitality.

In these rapidly changing times, it is all about principled choices and assumptions: idealism above opportunism, depth above superficiality, intimacy not just usefulness, creativity instead of taking the well-trodden paths, and servitude above egocentricity. This requires a conscious choice for a life guided by principles: honest, consistent, and convincing. This way of life offers inner stability. No matter what happens, you can always come home to yourself.

More of the same	*Different*
COMPETITIVE	**EXCELLING**
more	deep
better	sincere
faster	daring

On a collective level, we have to search for what binds and connects. An inspiring ambition level that clearly shows what service we provide for society and why it is worthwhile to share our joys and sorrows with each other. What's more, a shared dream or ideal acts as an adhesive for the ego. The most important thing, however, is that we have the courage to put the chosen ideals into practice, whatever the consequences of that may be.

This also applies to any other relationship: be sincere and trustworthy, don't speak about each other in each other's absence, be open about the your true motives, resolve issues of trust, and end an unfruitful relationship on time. And pay special attention to bringing together the right people, formulating the corporate identity and defining aims that make people enthusiastic, creating world-class processes and setting the right priorities.

In this way, a passionate culture can arise, in which people give the best of themselves and terms such as quality improvement, revitalization, entrepreneurial behavior, service and empowerment are given real content.

APPENDICES

We invite you to make use of the following diagnostic instruments to define for yourself where you are regarding your personal integrity and how you view organizations. Needless to say, *Be Honest* give your answers the value between 1–5, 5 =very much and 1 =very little. Tally your results, check the advice given below and share your conclusions with others. Continue to work towards improving your integrity and take the initiative to help your organization change with the times.

a. *Individual Integrity Mirror*

I communicate clearly and straight about my feelings and needs	1	2	3	4	5
My personal integrity and credibility takes pre-eminence over everything	1	2	3	4	5
I make public my feelings of pleasure and sorrow/anger	1	2	3	4	5
I experience inner rest and peace	1	2	3	4	5
Everybody knows where they stand with me	1	2	3	4	5
I cannot by trapped in telling "white lies"	1	2	3	4	5
I never make myself larger or smaller than I can justify from inside	1	2	3	4	5
There is enthusiasm and safety in my words and gestures	1	2	3	4	5
I am proud of who I am and what I represent	1	2	3	4	5
I always accept responsibility for my part in the situation	1	2	3	4	5

b. *Integrity Mirror for Organizations*

The identity of the organization is apparant in the behavior of all employees	1	2	3	4	5
The organizational aims are the psychological property of the employees	1	2	3	4	5
We learn from mistakes and criticism	1	2	3	4	5
The leadership is honest and is trusted	1	2	3	4	5
Employees think they are taken seriously and valued appropriately	1	2	3	4	5
Internal communication is characterized by openness and honesty	1	2	3	4	5
The customer/client understands clearly what he may expect	1	2	3	4	5
Employees feel free to discuss their cares and problems	1	2	3	4	5
There is trust about each others intentions and behavior	1	2	3	4	5
Agreements are always put into practice	1	2	3	4	5

Scores:

Number of points: (5 = high, 1 = low)	Total:
Maximum number of points: 50	Individual
Minimum number of points: 10	Organization

10–20: The gap between wish and reality has become so wide that you may shut your eyes to it. You need to take a good hard look at yourself.
20–30: Urgent need to do some soul searching, so that the great difference between "fiction" and reality is resolved.
30–40: Keep working consciously on more honest behavior. After six months, hold up the mirror again and evaluate.
40–50: There is a good chance that you work in an organization where, thanks to your sincere behavior, people do what they say and realize what they promise.

THREE EXAMPLES OF A CREDO

An organization's mission must give direction and meaning and at the same time bind people and make them enthusiastic. We found the following three examples:

Institute of Education, La Digue, Indian Ocean
"This school creates conditions that allow pupils and staff to grow in the path to excellence from valuing themselves and others, and to develop relationships based on honesty and mutual respect."

Ritz-Carlton Hotel Group
"The Ritz-Carlton hotel is a place where the genuine care and comfort of our guest is our highest mission. We pledge to provide the finest personal service and facilities for our guests who will always enjoy a warm, relaxed yet refined ambience. The Ritz-Carlton experience enlivens the senses, instills well-being, and fulfils even the unexpressed wishes and needs of our guests."

Or in all simplicity: "We are ladies and gentlemen serving Ladies and Gentlemen."

There is also a promise to the employees: "At The Ritz-Carlton, our Ladies and Gentlemen are the most important resource in our service commitment to our guests. By applying the principles of trust, honesty, respect, integrity and commitment, we nurture and maximize talent to the benefit of each individual and the company. The Ritz-Carlton fosters a work environment where diversity is valued, quality of life is enhanced, individual aspirations are fulfilled and the Ritz-Carlton mystique is strengthened."

A council organization

Our council organization is an efficient, honest, and innovative partner in maintaining, improving, and renewing the services offered by our council organization. We add value by strengthening and expanding our position as advisors to the Local Council, directors of the policy process, and suppliers of council services. The Council is an excellent employer and offers conditions to its employees that invite top performance in a result and service oriented context.

This council also laid down the following guidelines for guided autonomy:

1 The credo describes the way in which we want to stand in the world. Everybody is personally responsible for giving form and content to this and for adding his or her own energy and inspiration to it.
2 The leading principles in our interaction with each other are openness, sincerity, trust, transparency, and commitment to the public cause.
3 Everybody does not only concentrate on his or her own work, but also on the effects and added value for others, for the process chain, and for the final result.

4 We apply to the maximum a minimum of rules (principle of light-footed management).
5 It is the responsibility of every employee to create a work environment characterized by process-directed actions, discipline, and teamwork.
6 Decisions are taken at the lowest level possible. Every employee is given and takes the space to make decisions that are important to him or her. If required, such decisions are defended in an open and conscientious atmosphere.
7 Everybody is fully responsible for the quality of his or her own contribution. At all levels, people are expected to be sensitive to the political nature of policy making and execution processes and to report this promptly.
8 All employees have the right to be involved in the planning of work that is expected of them.
9 If there is any deviation from rules, procedures, agreements, and planning, then this must be reported as soon as the intention or the problem arises.
10 Be an ambassador for the council in all contacts, both within the local council area and outside it.
11 Improve the world and begin with yourself. Discuss concerns and differences of opinion with the person involved. Back-room politics poison the climate.

We came across the most extensive example of a chosen identity and the resulting rules of behavior in our small service organization. The process for arriving at this was just as important as the final result. The management defined the parameters (left column), which the employees then filled in and refined.

Corporate aims *(What do we want to achieve?)*		Cultural elements *(What elements must be present in our culture to allow this?)*	Behavioral criteria *(What elements of behavior are present in a believable role model within the culture?)*	Desired behavior
Continuity of the organization	Capable of adapting flexibly to the changing demands of the market	Continuously becoming more professional	• Initiative • Reflection • Ability to change	• Taking the initiative for self-training • Continuously involved in improvement and revitalization • Freeing time for product development and publications • Inter-vision
Innovative in professional area		Customer oriented; considerable attention to accountmanagement	• Aware of the surroundings • Listening • Power of conviction	• Up to date automation • Treat your customers as you would wish to be treated • Orderly and tidy surroundings, flowers • Non smoking • Take care of people: coffee when they arrive and later (fruit and cake)
Excellent service	Exceeding customers' expectations	Reliable; keeping agreements and appointments, walk the talk	Planning/progress control	• Account information in order • Give follow-up to contacts (after sales) • Better too quickly than too late • Adapting to the real needs of the customers • Exterior and design as good as possible

	An efficient and effective business policy / cost-conscious and-costeffective	Operating with vision and in accordance with agreed priorities	• Identification • Problem analysis • Judgment forming	• Keep an eye on business interests, but not at the cost of service • Be critical about (own) efficiency • Align operations with organization's identity
Real added value to the customer	Operating according to the existing social and professional norms	Personal and involved (no-nonsense with a heart)	• Sensitivity • Flexibility of style	• Show interest on your own initiative; even if there is no direct commercial interest involved • Honest, direct, and warm communi-cation • Aimed at opportunities, not at difficulties (positive and constructive approach) • Reliable and accessible information
Real added value for your own organization		• Teamspirit and collegiality • Open communication • Credibility (the behavior that is experienced by others is consistent with the underlying norms, values, ideas, and way of thinking) • Inspiring and refreshing performance	Co-operation	• Operating from a win-win mentality, aware of conscious wealth • Make interests and need explicit, and help others with this • Equal and really interested • Understanding the other is more important than being understood yourself • Sharing information • Learning from each other • Seeking help and support in time • Inner discipline

RECOMMENDED READING

Arbinger Institute. *Leadership and Self-Deception: Getting out of the Box.* Berrett-Koehler, San Francisco, 2000.

Barrett, Richard. *A Guide to Liberating Your Soul.* Fulfilling Books, Alexandria 1995.

Barrett, Richard. *Liberating the Corporate Soul: Building a Visionary Organization.* Butterworth-Heinemann, Boston 1998.

Bellman, Geoffrey M. *The Consultant's Calling: Bringing Who You Are to What You Do.* Jossey-Bass Publishers, San Francisco 1990.

Bellman, Geoffrey M. *Getting Things Done When You Are Not in Charge.* Fireside, San Francisco 1993.

Bellman, Geoffrey M. *Your Signature Path: Gaining New Perspectives on Live and Work.* Berrett-Koehler, San Francisco, 1996.

Bellman, Geoffrey M. *The Beauty of the Beast: Breathing New Life into Organizations.* Berrett-Koehler, San Francisco 2000.

Blanchard, Ken and Norman Vincent Peale. *The Power of Ethical Management.* William Morrow, New York 1988.

Blanchard, Ken and Sheldon Bowles. *Gung Ho! Turn On the People in Any Organization.* William Morrow, New York 1997.

Blanchard, Ken, John P. Carlos and Alan Randolph. *The 3 Keys to Empowerment: Release the Power Within People for Astonishing Results.* Berrett-Koehler, San Francisco 2001.

Block, Peter. *The Empowered Manager: Positive Political Skills at Work.* Jossey-Bass, San Francisco 1987.

Block, Peter. *Stewardship: Choosing Service over Self-Interest.* Berrett-Koehler, San Francisco 1993.

Block, Peter. *The Answer to How is Yes: Acting on What Matters.* Berrett-Koehler, San Francisco, 2002.

Bosch, Ingeborg. *Rediscovering the True Self.* www.pastrealityintegration.nl, 2002.

Bridges, William. *Making Sense of Life's Changes.* Perseus Publishing, New York 1980.

Collins, James and Jerry Porras. *Built to Last: Successful Habits of Visionary Companies.* HarperBusiness, New York 1994

Cooper, Robert. *Executive IQ: Emotional Intelligence in Business.* Orion Books, London 1997.

Cornelis, Arnold. *Logica van het gevoel: Filosofie van stabiliteitslagen van de cultuur als nesteling der emoties.* Essence, Middelburg 1998.

Cornelis, Arnold. *De vertraagde tijd: Revanche van de geest als filosofie van de toekomst.* Essence, Middelburg 1999.

Covey, Stephen R. *Principle-centered Leadership.* Summit Books New York 1990.

Crum, Thomas F. *Journey to Center: Lessons in Unifying Body, Mind, and Spirit.* Simon & Schuster, New York 1997.

Davis, John. *The Diamond Approach: An Introduction to the Teachings of A.H. Almaas.* Shambhala, Boston 1999.

Drath, Wilfred. *The Deep Blue Sea: Rethinking the Source of Leadership.* Jossey-Bass, San Francisco 2001.

Elliot, A. Larry and Richard Schroth. *How Companies Lie: Why Enron is Just the Tip of the Iceberg.* Nicholas Brealey Publishing, London 2002.

Freire, Paulo. *Pedagogy of the Oppressed.* Penguin Books, New York 1996.

Kerkhof, Twan van de. *Vragen voor de echte leider.* Bert Bakker, Amsterdam 1998.

Knoke, William. *Bold New World: The Essential Road Map to the Twenty-First Century.* Kodansha America, New York 1997.

Fijlstra, Rob and Harry Wullings. *No-nonsense met een hart.* Scriptum, Schiedam 1996.

Fijlstra, Rob and Harry Wullings. *Ondernemen met gevoel: Hoe persoonlijke en organisatie-ontwikkeling elkaar kunnen versterken.* Scriptum, Schiedam 1998.

Fukuyama, Francis. *The End of History and the Last Man.* Penguin Books, New York 1993.

Freiberg, Kevin and Jackie. *Nuts! Southwest Airlines' Crazy Recipe for Business and Personal Success*, Broadway Books, New York 1996.

Greenleaf, Robert. *Servant Leadership: A Journey into the Nature of Legitimate Power and Greatness.* Paulist Press, New York 1977.

Handy, Charles. *The Hungry Spirit; Beyond Capitalism: A Quest for Purpose in the Modern World.* Broadway books, New York 1998.

Japin, Arthur. *The Two Hearts of Kwasi Boachi.* Alfred A. Knopf, New York 2000.

Jaworski, Joseph. *Synchronicity: The Inner Path of Leadership.* Berrett-Koehler, San Francisco 1996.

Miller, Alice. *The Drama of the Gifted Child: The Search for the True Self.* Basic Books, New York 1996.

Moss Kanter, Rosabeth. *On the Frontiers of Management.* Simon & Schuster, New York 1997.

Kubler-Ross, Elisabeth. *The Wheel of Life: A Memoir of Living and Dying.* Scribner, New York 1997.

Owen, Harrison. *The Spirit of Leadership: Liberating the Leader in Each of Us.* Berrett-Koehler, San Francisco 1999.

Owen, Harrison. *The Power of Spirit: How Organizations Transform.* Berrett-Koehler, San Francisco 2000.

Pörksen, Uwe. *Plastikwörter: Die Sprache einer internationalen Diktatur*, Klett-Cotta, Stuttgart 1997.

Quinn, Robert E. *Deep Change: Discovering the Leader Within.* Jossey-Bass, San Francisco 1996.

Quinn, Robert E. *Change the World: How Ordinary People Can Achieve Extraordinary Results.* Jossey-Bass, San Francisco 2000.

Semler, Ricardo. *Maverick! The Success Story Behind the World's Most Unusual Workplace.* Times Books, New York 1993.

Swieringa, Joop and Bianca Elmers. *In plaats van reorganiseren.* Wolters-Noordhoff, Groningen 1996.
Treacey, Michael and Fred Wiersema. *The Discipline of Market Leaders: Choose Your Customers, Narrow Your Focus, Dominate Your Market.* Addison Wesley, Reading, Mass., 1995.
Thurow, Lester C. *The Future of Capitalism: How Today's Economic Forces Shape Tomorrow's World.* Penguin Books, New York 1997.
Thurow, Lester C. *Building Wealth: The New Rules for Individuals, Companies, and Nations in a Knowledge-Based Economy.* Harper Collins Publishers, New York 1999.
Weick, Karl. *Making Sense of the Organization.* Blackwell Publishers, New York 2000.
Wheatley, Margaret and Myron Kellner-Rogers. *A Simpler Way.* Berrett-Koehler, San Francisco 1995.
Wheatly, Margaret J. *Turning to One Another: Simple Conversations to Restore Hope to the Future.* Berrett-Koehler, San Francisco 2002.
Wierdsma, André. *Co-creatie van verandering.* Eburon, Delft 1999.
Zwart, Cees. *De strategie van de hoop.* Lemniscaat, Rotterdam 1998.